Your Child Is Defiant:
Why Is Nothing Working?

Your Child Is Defiant: Why Is Nothing Working?

Figure out the Cause and Then Choose Your Strategy

by

David Gottlieb, Ph.D.

ISBN 978-1-257-10859-6

Table of Contents

Acknowledgments

I want to thank a number of people who have helped me with this project. In the early stages Nancy Love, John Aherne, and Nancy Crossman gave me encouragement and advice. More recently Nancy Paul Gray of Woodbine House has shown interest in my book, and my agent Marian Betancourt has encouraged me to self-publish as a way to begin to make my book available to parents. Each of these people has felt the ideas in this book are important and not available in other books about defiant children.

My family has also given me encouragement and advice. My children Seth, Lev and Shira have listened to me talk about my ideas, and Seth has been instrumental in helping me market my book. My wife Fawn has read over the chapters more than once and made many helpful suggestions. Also thanks to Amaris and Matthew, and their parents Jan and Marni, for their help with the front cover.

I want to thank Dr. Alan Ravitz and Risa Graff for reading over my book and for writing such lovely endorsements, which you can find on the back cover. Also, a number of parents of the children I work with have read the manuscript and made positive comments. Thank you.

My patients have been a source of ideas for the book, and though I made sure to keep them anonymous, I want them to know that my ideas came together through working with them. My goal in this book is to transmit to others what I have learned in my clinical practice. Thirty years of working with children and parents have taught me to think carefully about what is going on with each child and family, and then to develop strategies that will help for each underlying problem.

Introduction

Why Is a Proper Assessment So Important?

Have you already tried to get tough with your defiant child? Have you already taken away all his privileges, and is he still not respecting your rules? Are you at your wit's end? Your emotions may swing from rage to hopelessness. You do not know what else to do. Do you sometimes wish you could send him, or her, somewhere else to live?

Seven Children Who Illustrate Defiant Behavior

We will follow seven families in this book who are struggling with what to do about their defiant children. Let me tell you first about Sam. Sam was fifteen and his parents were divorced. When he was at his mother's home, he would isolate himself in his bedroom. When the mother called him for dinner, he did not come downstairs, and eventually she went up to get him. She would tell Sam loudly it was dinner time, and Sam usually said or did nothing. The mother would then reach for his arm, and Sam would pull away but get out of bed and begin to make his way downstairs. Sometimes he had a few choice words, like "leave me alone, you b…"

One day Sam went into his brother's room to get his headphones. His mother saw him doing this and followed him into the room. She told him to put down the headphones, and said that he had to ask his brother if he could borrow them. Sam did not listen to his mother and walked out of his brother's room with the headphones. His mother became furious, yelled at Sam to put down the headphones, and followed him to his room. She stood in his room and refused to leave until Sam gave her the headphones. Sam proceeded to call her a swear word and push her away. Sam's defiance had escalated to using physical force, and his mother felt angry, but did not know what to do next. The following day, she called me.

Another child we will follow in this book is eight years younger than Sam, but the parents were also at their wit's end when they called me. Ginny was seven years old. She defied her parents when it was time to do homework and when it was time to go to bed. She refused to go to bed at 8 p.m. and would tell her parents she was not tired. If they insisted, she would begin whining. Her parents would then tell her to be quiet and get ready for bed, at which point Ginny would usually begin crying and refuse to move. What should the parents do? Why would Ginny struggle every night when it was bed time?

Ginny did not become physical with her parents, but she did sometimes call them "stupid," and similar to Sam, she refused to cooperate with her parents. A third child who also would not cooperate with his parents was a fourteen year old named Arthur. Arthur did not pay attention to many of his parents' rules. He would tease his younger brother, and did not listen to his mother's requests that he leave his brother alone. His mother explained to me that Arthur also would not obey her when it was time to do his homework, when it was time to come to dinner, or when it was time to get ready for bed. He either ignored her or told her to leave him alone. Once when the father was home to help and got stern with Arthur, he said to his dad "I hope you die." Usually Arthur just refused to obey his parents, but once in a while he became verbally hostile, like the day he told his father that he wished the dad were dead. The parents were alarmed by this behavior and asked me what they should do.

A fourth child we shall take a look at in this book is Donny, age eleven. Donny would go out of his way to irritate his older brother and sister while they were watching television or eating dinner. He would hum while the television was on or walk in front of the television so that his siblings had a hard time seeing their show. At the dinner table he made loud slurping noises on purpose. When the parents asked him to stop, Donny denied that he had done anything wrong. "I'm just eating" he would say. Sometimes there would be an ongoing discussion at the dinner table during which his siblings and his parents took turns confronting Donny about his obnoxious behavior. This did not help, and Donny became more and more argumentative. The parents called and asked me what to do.

A fifth child we will follow in the book is Felicia. Felicia was seventeen and had begun dating a young man who had no curfew and who was allowed to spend time with Felicia alone in his bedroom. Felicia's mother was appalled by this lack of supervision and feared that her daughter would have intercourse and get pregnant. Felicia had been respectful of her parents' rules until she began dating this young man. Now she argued several times a week with her mother because her mother refused to let her go out some days and because sometimes her mother made her get off the phone so that she would do her homework. Also, Felicia's mother insisted on an eleven o'clock curfew on weekends, and forbade her daughter from going to her boyfriend's house if his parents were out. The mother tried to talk with the boy's parents about her concerns, but they felt she was being silly. Felicia began to lie to her mother about where she was going, and became less helpful around the house. Arguments between them increased and led to instances of crying by the mother and/or daughter. The mother asked me what she should do.

Another child I will discuss is Daniel age eleven who erupted into hour-long rages when he did not get to do something he was expecting. For example, one day in the car he asked his mom to stop at a fast food restaurant for lunch, and he thought she would say yes. When she said not now, Daniel exploded with anger. He was sitting in the back seat of the car and began kicking her seat, and even tried to open the car door to get out while the car was moving. Luckily Daniel could not open the car door; and the mom pulled the car over to the curb and waited for almost an hour for Daniel to calm down enough for her to continue driving. Other days, Daniel's anger might not last as long, but he would still usually be loud and aggressive when he did not get to do what he wanted. With Daniel's increasing size, the mother was worried she would not be able to stop him much longer from hurting himself or someone else. She did not know what to do.

The last example I will give you is of a teenager age sixteen, named George, who disregarded many of his parent's rules. Like Felicia he lied about where he was going in the evenings. However, he was not going out to see a girlfriend, but to hang out with his buddies and drink beer. One night they had been drinking in a local park and the police found them. Charges were filed in the juvenile courts. Another major problem was that he sometimes stole food from a convenience store, and one day the store owner caught him and called his parents. When his parents grounded him for drinking or for stealing, he did not argue. He told them that he did not care what they said, that he was going to continue to go out anyway whenever he felt like it. The parents could not block the door. Could they do anything to turn George around?

These examples illustrate that there is a range of defiant behavior. In each case, the parent has made a request of the child, and the child has not cooperated. Some children throw tantrums when asked to do something, and others are lawyerlike in their arguments. There are also some children who will not argue with you, but ignore what you have to say. They may even walk away while you are speaking. All of the children I have mentioned above defied their parents on a daily basis. In each case, the parents had already consulted their family doctor. Ginny and Arthur were on ADHD medication. The medication had made no difference in their behavior toward their parents. Several of the parents had also tried behavior modification techniques (rewards and punishments) to no avail. All the parents were frustrated and did not know what to do next.

Something else needed to be done. Most parenting books offer one approach for all defiant children, often involving some combination of rewards and punishments. What happens when the approach does not work for your child? Did you do something wrong? Or is your child just worse than other children? You worry that your family life will always be a struggle.

Chart I: Where To Find Out More About the Seven Children Introduced in This Chapter

	Chapters
Sam	1, 6, 7, 8
Ginny	1, 4, 5, 7, 8
Arthur	1, 4
Donny	1, 3, 9
Daniel	1, 6
Felicia	1, 3, 7, 8, 9
George	1, 6

A Careful Assessment Will Guide You Toward a Solution

This book, *Your Child Is Defiant: Why Is Nothing Working?*, will help you figure out what is underlying your child's defiance. There are many pathways that lead to defiant behavior, and each pathway requires a different solution. One size does not fit all! In *Why Is Nothing Working?* you will learn how to assess your child's problem so that you can come to a proper decision about what to do. You will learn the key diagnostic issues which a psychologist considers in order to decide on the proper course of action. The book will help you avoid false starts so that you do not have to go through additional months with your child screaming, arguing or defying your rules.

Defiance in children and adolescents can take several forms. The way the child misbehaves can vary depending on the child's mood and personality. Some children are louder and more aggressive than others. Also, a child's mood can vary during the day, and his expression of disobedience can likewise vary. At times when your child is more energized, he is likely to express his defiance more vehemently. When your child is calm or withdrawn, he is more likely to ignore you.

Furthermore, there can be differences in the duration and frequency of defiant behavior. Some children are defiant many times a day, and others only several times a week. Each occurrence can last a few minutes or an hour or more. In either case, parents can become frustrated and wonder what they have to do in order to get their child to respect their rules. Parents want to know: How do I get my child to listen to me?

You cannot decide on an approach to your child's defiance until you first understand what is bringing it about. Many parenting books are geared toward one type of child: a strong-willed or oppositional child who has no other personal or family problems. In these cases, traditional parenting books which focus on discipline techniques can be helpful. However, in my experience, more than half of defiant children have some other cause underlying their behavior. The approach of current parenting books will not be of much help then.

My book will take you through the steps necessary to figure out the cause of your child's defiance. The two chapters of the first section introduce you to the way a psychologist assesses a problem like defiance. I will show you how to observe carefully what is going on, and I will explain what questions you need to answer in order to decide what is causing your child to misbehave.

Each chapter in the second section of the book examines the possible causes of defiance and explains what you should do in each case to change your child's behavior. I will show you which techniques work for each possible cause. The chapters in this section (chapters three through seven) will begin with an assessment question. Your answers to the questions will help you decide whether this chapter is relevant to your child and will help you narrow down your child's underlying problem. Each chapter will explain a different pathway or cause of defiant behavior. More important, I will then show you what you can do to help your child if he has the problem in question.

As I discuss each cause of defiance and then explain the approach you should use, it will become clear how the cause and solution go hand in hand. Making this connection is what is unique about my book compared to other books about defiance. Other books focus on only one cause and tell you what to do only for that issue. What if your child does not have that underlying problem? Then the suggestions will not be helpful. One size does not fit all!

In addition to starting each of these chapters with an assessment question, I will also include at the beginning of a chapter a boxed off section that serves like a roadmap for that chapter. It will give you a preview of what the chapter will discuss. Each of these chapters will also come with two kinds of charts. One type will highlight the key information parents need to know to make a correct assessment. The other chart will summarize the key techniques you should use for each cause of defiance. At the end of each of these chapters, I will also present a list of "what to do and what not to do", if your child has the problem in question. The list will give you a number of concrete suggestions so that you know exactly how to change your child's behavior.

Throughout the book there will be many examples presented from my clinical practice. No identifying information will be used so that people's identity remains confidential. We will follow the seven children I have introduced in this chapter in the rest of the book. Briefer descriptions of other children will also be used to illustrate key points. The goal is to make it clear to you what you need to do for each possible cause of defiance.

Toward the end of the book, I will explain what you can do for more complicated cases. For some children, you will find that there are multiple causes of defiance. In chapter eight, I will explain what you should do then. I will show you when to address one cause before the other, and when you will need to work on both causes at the same time.

In chapter nine, I will explain that in some cases, a new diagnosis emerges as you gather more information. Sometimes a past trauma, like physical or sexual abuse, is discovered. While this is the not a common cause of defiance in children, I will explain what you should do if it has occurred. Finally, at the end of the book I will point you toward other resources that can help. There are a number of useful books and websites for particular causes of defiance, and I will mention some of them in the last chapter of my book.

If you want professional help, I will also explain in the last chapter how to go about finding the right mental health professional for your child. Particularly if your child has been defiant over a long period of time, it may be useful to consult with a clinician to get additional advice. Also, if there are multiple causes of defiance or if there has been a major trauma in your child's life, it would probably be helpful to have a professional work with you and your child. My book will help you figure out what to do to help your child, but at times it is hard for parents to do it all by themselves. Do not be embarrassed to ask your child's teacher, other parents, or professionals for assistance.

In this book, my goal is to help you figure out why your child is behaving the way he is and then show you how the correct approach fits with the assessment you have made. This is the first book that offers a step-by-step assessment procedure for parents and also ties the corrective actions to your analysis of the problem. Only if parents take a step back and determine what are the causes of their child's behavior will they be able to make the right decisions. In the next chapter, I will start you on the way toward figuring out what is going on with your child.

Chapter 1

The First Step Is Careful Observation

> Careful observation of your child's defiant behavior is one key to helping you figure out the cause. You need to observe the sequence of behaviors which lead up to your child's defiance as well as what your child actually says and does when he is defiant. Furthermore, you should note with whom your child is defiant. All these observations will help you figure out what is going on with your child. This chapter will explain in detail what you need to observe in your family.

Observe "About What" and "With Whom" Your Child Is Angry

Before you can figure out how to help your defiant child, it is very important that you carefully observe his, or her, behavior. You need to look at what is happening when your child becomes defiant. Specifically focus on these two questions: 1) *What* is your child upset about, and 2) With *whom* is your child interacting at the time? These two questions help you focus on the specifics of what your child is reacting to.

As you think about what happened, try to be as objective as you can. It is natural for you to feel frustrated and believe your child spins out of control so often that it hardly matters what happened before he became defiant. But something precipitated the outburst, and it is important to think about what was going on when the outburst occurred. These details will help us figure out why your child is behaving this way. Try to think about the situation from your child's perspective as well as your own. Think about how you would explain what happened in a factual way to someone who was not there. Basically, describe the sequence of events: what did the adult say or do, and what did your child say or do.

I would like you to write down your observations each time your child becomes defiant over the next week. This record will help you to see if there are any patterns. I would also like you to think about what was happening during the hour before your child became defiant. You may not always remember exactly what happened, but if you can, I'd like you to write a sentence summarizing what your child and the "target" adult (the adult with whom the child was defiant) were doing in the hour leading up to the incident. Sometimes this provides useful information about the cause of the child's defiance.

Keeping a Written Record

Here's the information I'd like you to record in the coming week:

Date:

Who was the target adult?

What did the target adult say or do, if anything, before your child was defiant?

What did your child say or do that was defiant?

What, if anything, did the adult say or do next?

What, if anything, did the child say or do next?

What was your child doing in the previous hour?

What was the target adult doing in the previous hour?

You can use a format like the following (chart 1.1) so that all your information is organized on one or two pages. Note that the target adult may be different in different examples.

Chart #1.1: Examples of Your Child's Defiant Behavior:

Scenario 1: Date_____

Who was the target adult?_____

What did the target adult say?

_____

_____

_____

What did your child say or do?

_____

_____

What did the adult say or do next?

_____

_____

_____

What did your child say or do next?

_____

_____

_____

What was your child doing in the hour preceding the above interaction?

_____

_____

_____

What was the target adult doing in the preceding hour?

_____

_____

Scenario 2: Date_____

Who was the target adult?_____

What did the target adult say?

_____

_____

_____

What did your child say or do?

_____

_____

What did the adult say or do next?

_____

_____

_____

What did your child say or do next?

_____

_____

_____

What was your child doing in the hour preceding the above interaction?

_____

_____

_____

What was the target adult doing in the preceding hour?

_____

_____

_____

Scenario 3: Date_____

Who was the target adult?_____

What did the target adult say?

_____
_____
_____

What did your child say or do?

_____
_____

What did the adult say or do next?

_____
_____
_____

What did your child say or do next?

_____
_____
_____

What was your child doing in the hour preceding the above interaction?

_____
_____
_____

What was the target adult doing in the preceding hour?

_____
_____

If the defiant behavior continues over a period of some minutes, try to record the main statements made by the adult and by your child in the sequence in which they occurred. If the adult made a request, and the child replied, and this led to further remarks by each, try to jot down how the conversation went. Feel free to extend your notes beyond the spaces I gave you in the chart. If the interaction went on for a long time and you can't write it all down, pay particular attention to what was said right before your child started to get angry. What did the target adult say before your child responded defiantly?

You may be asking yourself now if you really have to write down all the examples of defiance over a week's time. You may feel you already know what the child and target adult will say. Or you may feel your child is defiant so often that it will take too long to write down every instance over a week's time. It would be useful to make at least three or four observations of when your child becomes defiant, though you will have even better information if you keep a whole week's record. It will help you to know for sure what happens in specific situations, rather than rely upon your memory which can at times be selective. We all tend to leave out some things when we remember past events.

Look for Patterns

After you have recorded the information over a week's time, you should look over everything to see if any patterns or themes emerge. Are there certain situations or certain people with whom your child is defiant? Does it happen with certain people more than others? What is the role of these people in your child's life? Are they the main authority figures? Furthermore, what is usually being asked of your child at the time? For example, if your child is defiant when you ask him to do his homework one day and when you ask him to do a chore another day, you might think these are two different problems. Or you might think that the common theme is that your child doesn't like to be asked to do anything work-related. Then you notice that in both situations he has been playing video games in the hour before you asked him to do something. If he has not been playing video games, he is less argumentative, though not perfectly compliant. You realize that the problem has to do with switching gears from video games to a less preferred task. You have found the "common denominator," or the common thread.

Sometimes the common denominator is the particular adult with whom your child is defiant. That does not mean it is the adult's fault. There can be various reasons why a child argues with one adult more than another. Sometimes the reason is that one adult is the main disciplinarian, and thus the child reacts more to him. In other families, one adult may be shy and retiring by nature, and not like to set limits. The child may think he can take advantage of this adult. I will help you decide the cause of your child's defiance in the coming chapters, but first you must carefully observe the circumstances when your child gets upset. Without knowing who the child is angry toward, and without knowing the situations where this occurs, it will be difficult to figure out the underlying problem. So keep a detailed record of what is going on when your child is defiant. Now let me tell you more about the seven children I introduced in the first chapter, and let's see what some of the common denominators are for those children:

Sam

Sam is the rebellious teen who was defiant primarily with his mother. Sometimes he was passive-aggressive and did not answer her questions, and sometimes he erupted and pushed her. Let's look further at what Sam and his mother said to each other at the time Sam was defiant. Often the mother had asked Sam a question about his activities. She asked about what he did with his friends, or what he did in school. If he did not answer, she sometimes said sarcastically: "Have you been smoking marijuana?" Sam would then become more aggressive in his response, sometimes shouting "no." He would often then go to his room, and his mother would sometimes follow and ask more questions. If she pursued him, Sam usually got louder.

Another source of conflict was dinner time. Sam was passive-aggressive when the mother said it was time for dinner. He refused to come downstairs to the kitchen table. The mother would scream for him to come downstairs, and he would ignore her. Sometimes the mother went up to his room and told Sam to come down immediately. Sam would usually be lying in bed, but when his mother came upstairs and stood by his bed or reached for his arm, he would get up. When she saw him get out of bed, she went back downstairs, and he followed a minute later.

There was one situation in which Sam's defiance escalated into pushing his mother. The problem began when Sam went into his brother's room and took his brother's headphones while his brother was not home. Mom saw this happen and asked Sam to put them back, but Sam refused and went to his room. Mom followed him and yelled at him to put the headphones back, and got real close to Sam. Sam yelled at her to leave. She said not until you give me the headphones. At this point, Sam pushed her. This was a difficult situation for the mother. She was very hurt and angry. Sam was as tall as her and stronger physically. She did not feel comfortable calling the divorced father for help, because the two of them had not been getting along well. Below you can see how this interaction was recorded using the chart I introduced earlier. The chart shows in a concrete way how the interaction went back and forth with Sam and his mother, each digging in their heels before Sam pushed her. Is there a way the mother could have avoided the back and forth escalation of anger with her son and still have had her son respect her wishes? And what should the mother do when her son pushes her? In later chapters I will explain what she can do to improve the outcome.

Sam's defiance actually increased on the days when the mother and father had been arguing. This connection became clear after we talked about what was going on in the hour before the pushing incident happened. There had been a major dispute between the parents that Sam had overheard. It is important therefore to think about what happened in the previous hour. Sometimes you can get important clues about what may be bothering your child. In this case, it was an argument between the parents. In another case, it may be that a child's patience wears thin waiting for a parent to arrive at a little league baseball game. Or your child may become frustrated while he is doing his homework, but not erupt until you ask him a question at the dinner table. If you do not observe what was happening in the hour leading up to your child's outburst, you may overlook what caused your child's defiance to escalate.

Chart #1.2: Charting One Example of Sam's Behavior with His Mother

Scenario 1: Date: _____after school one day

Who was the target adult? _____the mother

What did the target adult say? _____Mom asked Sam to put back his brother's headphones

What did your child say or do? _____Sam said no and walked to his room

What did the adult say or do next? _____Mom followed Sam to his room and yelled "Put those headphones back."

What did your child say or do next? _____ Sam yelled at her to get out of his room.

What did the adult say or do next? _____Mom said not until you give me the headphones back.

What did your child say or do next? _____Sam pushed his mother toward the door.

What was your child doing in the hour preceding the above interaction? _____Sam overheard his parents having a heated argument about his grades and about why his father wasn't doing more to discipline him.

What was the target adult doing in the preceding hour? _____The mother had a heated argument with Sam's father about Sam's grades and about the father's lack of rules.

Ginny

Another child I introduced in the first chapter was Ginny. She is seven, and she did not start her homework when asked and did not get ready for bed at the correct time. First she would ignore her parents' requests, and when they asked again she would say "no, leave me alone." Sometimes she would start to cry. If it was bedtime, she would add that she was not tired, or if she was asked to do her homework, she would say that she had done it after school at her grandmother's house. Parents knew this was not the case, so they insisted she sit down with them to do the homework. Sometimes they had to yell to get her to start her homework or to get ready for bed. Ginny would often scream as well: "leave me alone."

Notice that in this case, similar to Sam, Ginny first ignored her parents' requests and then became increasingly verbal as the parents insisted. But in a number of other ways Ginny acted differently than Sam. She did not become physical, and also she would carry on with both parents, not just the mother. Further, Ginny's defiance was limited primarily to homework and bedtime. Unlike Sam, she would answer questions about her day, and come to dinner on time. Since her defiance was limited to certain situations, it is important to figure out why these were issues for Ginny. In the following chapters you will discover why Ginny reacted the way she did at homework time and at bedtime. For Sam, you will find out why he reacted so strongly to any request by his mother, but not by his father.

Arthur

Arthur was the fourteen year old who did not cooperate with his parents when it was time to move form one activity to the next, whether it was time to come to dinner, to take a shower, to get ready for bed, or to start his homework. He was usually passive-aggressive and ignored his parents at first. When the parents insisted, he either continued to ignore them, or said "I'll do it later." The parents would then say "now" and Arthur usually said "I'm busy." By about the fifth time the parents said something, Arthur would get up and act like he was going to get started. Parents would often have to follow him and say again to put down what he was doing (often reading a book or magazine). Eventually, Arthur did what the parents had asked, but the whole process would be repeated the next time they asked Arthur to do something.

Arthur was similar to Sam in some ways. Neither boy said much; both initially defied an adult by ignoring the adult's request. The difference is that Sam only avoided his mother, while Arthur avoided requests made by both his parents. Furthermore, Sam was often in a foul mood whenever his mother was around, whereas Arthur was happy at home as long as he was not being asked to stop what he was doing.

Occasionally Arthur became verbally hostile toward his father. In one example, Arthur was not listening to his mother's requests to take a shower, and the father yelled that he had had enough and that Arthur "better get upstairs right this minute." Arthur screamed back at his father "I hope you die." During the hour preceding this hostile remark, there were no signs that Arthur was upset. His anger was triggered when his father got exasperated and yelled that he had had enough. Why did Arthur become more verbally hostile with his father than his mother? One possibility is the difference in the way the two adults reacted to Arthur's defiance. The mother hardly yelled, and when she did Arthur did not seem intimidated. While the father did not yell often, when he did, it was quite loud and forceful according to the rest of the family. Arthur's statement that "I hope you die" came after the father was particularly loud and insistent.

Donny

The fourth child I introduced in the last chapter was Donny, an eleven year old. His defiance only began in the last few months. One situation where there was trouble was dinner time. He would make slurping noises at the table, particularly when his older brother or sister was speaking. When the parents told him to stop, he denied that he had done anything wrong. If his parents continued speaking with him about it, Donny would argue that his parents were picking on him. No matter what the parents said to explain their point of view, Donny argued that they weren't being fair. In addition, Donny had begun arguing with the parents when they asked him to do his homework. He would tell them he'd do it later, and asked why they didn't trust him. He'd continue complaining, until the parents left the room. The parents didn't know what had gotten into Donny, because he had been pretty compliant until the last few months. This case of defiance is different than the others we have considered. First, it was of recent origin, while the others had been going on for a year or more. Secondly, Donny talked about feeling the parents did not care about him or trust him. What was underlying this reaction from Donny? You will find out in chapter three, which is about situational causes of defiance.

Daniel

Daniel was also eleven years old, but his acts of defiance were more aggressive and longer lasting. He often yelled loudly and sometimes became physical, kicking a door, or throwing an object at a wall. He did not strike his parents. Even when he was in a rage, he seemed to know this was forbidden. In the introduction, I told you about one example of his anger when he did not get to eat at a fast food restaurant as he had expected. He began kicking the seat in the car where his mother was sitting. The mother reported that Daniel would become physically aggressive once every week or two. By charting the aggressive behaviors, we figured out that preceding an outburst he was extremely disappointed about not being able to do something that he very much wanted to do *and* that he thought he was going to be able to do. Often what he had wanted, like to eat at a fast food restaurant, were things that the parents indeed had done with him many times in the past, but were unable or unwilling to do all the time.

There were other times during a typical day when Daniel got quite angry (often swearing), but he was not physically aggressive, and the anger did not last as long, usually fifteen minutes or less (which is still a long time if you are the parents listening to his provocative and nasty words). One regular time of conflict was with homework. Unlike Ginny, the work was not particularly difficult for Daniel. However, Daniel would rather play video games, and when his parents told him he had to stop and do his homework, Daniel often refused at first and yelled at them to leave him alone. He or his parents would eventually turn off the game, and after about fifteen minutes he would calm down and usually begin his homework. Daniel often rushed through the work though, and when the parents checked it over, they noticed that some answers were left out, and some answers were hard to read. When they asked him to fix his work, Daniel often refused. The parents usually insisted, unless it was close to bedtime. After some whining about how the parents were "slave drivers" he complied. The parents were often exhausted by bedtime! Dealing with Daniel after coming home from work was draining.

Felicia

The sixth child we will follow is Felicia, a seventeen year old teenager who was not defiant until she became attached to her boyfriend. She wanted to see him every day if possible, and she wanted to be alone with him. Felicia's mother would not allow her to go out every day, so that when this issue came up after she got home from school there was often a loud confrontation that ended in tears by mother and/or daughter.

The argument usually went like this: The daughter said her mother was worrying for nothing and was interfering in her life. The mother would reply "You are still my daughter, and I make the rules. School is your number one priority, not this boy." The girl would respond that she was handling school well and wanted to see her boyfriend for a little while after school. The mother said her grades could be better, and that she was only saying no to her going out because she loved her. Some days Felicia would turn away, go up to her room, and slam the door, and other days she began yelling that the mother was being unfair. The mother would yell back that the daughter was under the spell of her boyfriend. At this point usually one or the other would begin crying, and the argument ended. The daughter did not push the issue and leave the house. However, she would sometimes lie on weekends: she would say she was going out with her girlfriends, but really go to her boyfriend's house.

Felicia's defiance, like Donny's, was of recent origin. She had mostly been a compliant child, and was close to her mother. Felicia also knew that her mother cared about her, which is different than how Donny felt. He thought his parents were not interested in him. Also, Felicia did not push the conflict to the point of physical confrontation, as Sam had done, nor did she swear. Felicia was mad because she felt her mother was too controlling. You will find out more about Felicia and her mother in chapter three.

George

It was harder to figure out the trigger for George's defiance. It had been going on for several years now. He defied his parents about curfew several nights a week. It was at night that he sometimes drank or stole food from a local convenience store. The drinking and stealing always occurred out of the house so the parents did not know how to stop it. They tried grounding him, but George left the house anyway. In this way he was more rebellious than Felicia, who usually became emotional and went up to her room. Notice that George did not get in a rage though like Daniel; he just said defiantly that he was going to do whatever he wanted. The one pattern the parents observed was that he always hung out with the same three friends in the evenings. When he violated curfew or drank, it was always with his same buddies.

One night he and his buddies drank in a park and were caught by the police. Now George was going to have to answer to a juvenile officer and a judge. The parents' first impulse was to try to prevent the case from going before a judge. But they noticed George was concerned about what the judge might do to him, and he did not seem to drink as much in the evenings any longer. They realized it might have been a good thing ultimately that he was caught by the police.

George also had a problem with going to school. He was frequently tardy because he would go somewhere to smoke cigarettes, and sometimes also marijuana. A few times he skipped school altogether and hung out with his friends at one of their houses. The parents found an empty baggie in his room with what looked like flakes of marijuana. When confronted about the pot and about skipping school, George did not deny it. But he said he would smoke when he felt like it. He also said he hated school and needed a day off sometimes. The parents said they were going to ground him for a week. George replied that he would go out when he felt like it. Interestingly when he got high and skipped school he was with the same groups of guys he hung out with in the evening. The school had suspended him and his friends a couple of times, but George did not seem to care about this. For George, it was like having another day off from school!

Summary

In this chapter, we have begun to gather data about each child's defiance. You can begin to see why getting the specific details about *what* was said to *whom* is so important. You will get clues from the information you gather. Sometimes the clues point to a probable cause of your child's defiance. For example, with Sam, we think that the parents' arguing with each other made Sam's defiance toward the mother escalate. With Ginny, we know it had something to do with bedtime and homework, but we do not know yet why these two issues were particular problems for Ginny. Arthur had trouble shifting gears from one activity to another, and became defiant at these times. Why was this so hard for Arthur? For Donny, we wonder why he had recently become defiant. Did it have something to do with his feeling that his parents did not seem to care about him? For Daniel, he was most angry when he could not do something that he was looking forward to and that he had been able to do in the past. Why did Daniel have such difficulty dealing with disappointment? Why did not going to a fast food restaurant bring on a violent explosion in the car that could have caused someone to be injured? For Felicia, we feel pretty sure the defiance had to do with her wanting to spend more time with her boyfriend. Were there any other contributing factors to this struggle between mother and daughter? And with George, the problems with drinking, stealing and smoking marijuana all occurred when he was with his friends. But how could the parents stop him from seeing his friends? And why did George disregard what his parents had to say?

There is other information you will need to gather before you can come up with a definite cause for your child's behavior. I will outline the questions you need to answer in the upcoming chapter. Careful observation of the times your child is defiant is the first step toward narrowing down what is going on with your child. You get clues, but not usually the complete answer. In the following chapters you will gather some more information until you come up with the answer. It's almost like what a detective does to solve a mystery. The fact finding is very important because you cannot treat every child who is defiant the same way. You need to know what is causing your child to act the way he is, and then you can determine what you need to do.

Chapter 2

Questions To Help You Figure Out the Cause

This chapter is an overview of the questions which you should ask yourself in order to figure out the cause of your child's defiance. A correct assessment is key, so take your time in thinking about these questions, and be sure to consider the opinions of other adults who know your child well, such as your spouse and your child's teachers. In subsequent chapters, we will consider one cause at a time and explain what you should do for each possible cause of your child's defiant behavior.

A Key Diagnostic Question Is When Did the Problems Start?

Now that you have observed and charted your child's defiant behavior over about a week's time, think about when this problem started. When did it start becoming an issue in your family? Think about how long you have had trouble getting your child to listen to what you want. The defiance may not have always been expressed in exactly the same way. When your child was younger, between the ages of three and eight, he may have had a lot of tantrums when you didn't let him watch his favorite videos, when you insisted he stop playing with his toys, or when he had to go to sleep. No one of these behaviors by itself is necessarily abnormal, but if on a daily basis there were many situations where you have had trouble getting your child to cooperate, and this went on for weeks or months, then you could conclude that your child's defiance was significant at a young age.

If your child's defiance did not begin when he was quite that young, think about whether there were signs as he got older, between the ages of nine and eighteen. The ways in which your child defies you may change as he gets older. There may be fewer temper tantrums, but more arguments, or your child may defy you by simply refusing to get up and do what you ask. If you press him to do his chores or to do his homework, he may become nasty or in some instances he may even begin yelling at you. As you look back, you realize you have been fighting these battles with your child for a year or more.

Contrast that scenario with one in which your child has generally been compliant over the years. During most of his childhood, your child has cooperated with doing his homework, and has not given you a hard time when you have needed him to be ready to go somewhere, like to school, church, or a relative's house. It is only recently, in the last few months, that your child has refused to listen to what you ask, or only recently that he argues or yells.

Situational Causes

If the problem began in the last few months, then something has likely changed in your child's life recently. What was going on in your child's life around the time that his defiance started? Think specifically about whether something changed. You might want to talk this over with your spouse or any other adult who knows your child well. If your child is willing to talk about his thoughts, you might ask him whether there have been any changes lately in school or at home. He may be willing to tell you if anything is bothering him. His perspective may not be entirely accurate or objective, but still it will give you clues about what might be affecting him. For example, he might say that his younger brother has been annoying him, while it seems to you the brother is acting no differently than normal. Your child's mentioning of the brother could still be a clue about what is bothering him. In one family that I was seeing, the younger brother was playing on a little league team and doing very well. The family was going to every game and bringing the older brother along. It became clear in our family meetings that what was bothering the older child was that he was not being admired in the same way as his sibling. What was truly annoying him therefore was not the brother's behavior toward him, as he had mentioned to the parents. Instead it was the parents' not noticing him as much. (At least in his mind there was a change.) The child's defiant behavior was a way to get some of the attention focused back on him.

When there are recent changes that affect your child's behavior, we label these causes "situational." We use this term because your child has not always been defiant. Rather there is a recent situation which has brought about your child's negative behavior.

There are generally two kinds of situational changes that can bring on defiant behavior. One is a loss of some kind and the other is growth or maturation of your child. The word "loss" refers not just to the death or moving away of key family members or friends, but also any changes in a parent's emotional availability, which the child experiences as a loss of emotional support. For example, when a parent starts a new job, he, or she, may have to be away for longer hours, or even if the parent comes home at the same time, he may be worn out by the new challenges at work. The child may recognize that the parent does not seem as interested in talking or playing in the evenings. Maybe the parent does not ask the same questions about school, does not watch television together with the child, or does not have much time to play a game. Your child may not be able to verbalize what is different, but he senses the change, and feels a sense of loss. Your child may become angry and defiant in reaction to these changes.

Sometimes it is not a loss but a maturational change that brings on defiant behavior. There are developmental changes at different ages which can cause stress for children and for their families. For example, some children, especially in the primary grades, may want to stay home rather than go to school. They feel anxiety about leaving their parents, and some of these children become defiant when parents tell them to get ready for school in the morning. The cause is anxiety about a developmental change; the children have reached the age where they are expected to separate for a good part of the day and go to school, but they feel so attached to their parents that they do not want to separate from them.

There are a number of other changes in the life of a family which can cause a child to become defiant. I will review these situational causes in the next chapter. I will also explain how you can lessen the effect of these changes and thereby reduce your child's defiance.

Structural Causes

If your child has been defiant for a long time, a year or longer, then the cause is less likely situational. We use the term "structural" to refer to causes that have existed for a long time. There may be some long term characteristic of your child that causes defiance. There could also be something about the structure of your family that underlies your child's defiant behavior.

Let's start with your child's characteristics. We need to consider your child's intellectual make-up, his social abilities, his personality type, and his emotional functioning. All four of these areas need to be examined in our search for a long term cause of your child's defiance.

Let me now introduce some key questions you need to ask about the first two of these long term characteristics: your child's intellectual ability and social skills. Depending on your answers to the following questions, your approach to your child's defiance will be different. First ask yourself if your child likes to interact with his peers. Does he have at least one good friend? If not, it is possible your child has an autistic disorder, and I will explain more about this in chapter four. I will explain what autism is and how it can bring on defiant behavior in children.

The next question to ask yourself is whether your child consistently struggles in at least one class in school. Is your child in danger of failing one or more of his classes? If so, one possible cause is that your child has a learning disability, and I will define different types of learning disabilities in chapter four. Children with learning problems become defiant because the work is so hard for them that they struggle with you about starting their homework. The work is frustrating and they would rather not attempt it. However, their teachers and parents urge them not to give up and to try harder. These children are unable to explain why the work is too hard, and often get angry at their parents and teachers.

If you rule out serious academic and social disorders, you should then consider whether your child's personality is the issue. What kind of personality is more likely to lead to defiant behavior? A key characteristic is being strong-willed (or headstrong). These children have strong opinions and do not like to defer to adults. Is your child sometimes insistent on doing things his way, even when you ask him repeatedly to do things in a different fashion? If your child insists on his approach, there is a greater likelihood that your child will become defiant if you try to set some limits. If, in addition, your personality is on the shy side, it may be difficult for you to set effective limits. Your child may sense that you will back off if he is defiant. I will discuss what you can do if your child is headstrong in chapter five.

In chapter six, I will explain what to do if your child is more hostile and argumentative than a headstrong child would be. Does your child seem to argue with you no matter what you have asked of him? What do you do if your child has frequent severe confrontations with adults? I will review the types of emotional disorders that defiant children can have, and discuss how your approach would vary depending on the disorder. Three disorders which could underlie a child's defiant behavior are oppositional defiant disorder, conduct disorder, and bipolar disorder.

While oppositional children can dig in their heels and argue with you as if they were trained lawyers, conduct disorder children may avoid you altogether, whereas bipolar children are more emotional and can have explosive tempers. Each type of underlying problem requires a different approach. If you or your doctor does not figure out the correct diagnosis, you will not know which approach to use.

One clue that your child may have a long term, structural problem can come from an examination of your family tree. Consider what you were like as a child, and also consider the behavior of your siblings, your parents, your aunts and uncles, and your nieces and nephews. Many structural features of a child's make-up have a genetic component so that you might expect to find some other example(s) in your family tree. Does someone else have a strong-willed personality or possibly an emotional disorder which is similar to your child's problem? Or is there a family history of learning disabilities or autism? These problems will often show up in some part of your family tree. If so, this adds weight to your suspicion that your child may have inherited a structural problem and that this problem could be underlying his defiant behavior. If you remember your brother yelling a lot at your mother many years ago when you were a child, it is very possible that your child's defiant behavior may be related. Maybe your brother was strong-willed like your child is. It is possible, though not certain, that their behaviors have the same genetic origin. The finding in your family tree gives added weight to the probability that there is a structural cause for your child's behavior.

In some cases, the cause of a child's defiance is not the make-up of his personality or a situational change in his life, but instead the problem may lie in the structure of your family. There may be long term conflicts or continual tension between the parents that can lead to the child's defiant behavior. If there are frequent, ongoing disputes between you and your spouse, your child may challenge you in the same way that your spouse does. Your child may think: "If Mom or Dad speaks that way, then so can I." It is important to look at what is going on in the relationships in the family, because any ongoing problems in the family can bring on defiance in children. In chapter seven, I will show you what to look out for in your family, and what you can do to improve family relationships.

One other question to ask yourself is whether you or your spouse has an emotional or substance abuse problem? If one of you does have a problem, you may unwittingly behave in a way that causes your child to be angry or defiant. One father of a defiant child I have seen in my office has been a binge drinker for years, but denies that his problem has anything to do with his son's defiance. However, when the father drinks, he becomes extremely critical and even challenges his son at times to a fight. The father does not usually remember his aggressive behavior when he is sober. Typically adults who have substance abuse problems act erratically at times, and this can cause stress and defiance in their children.

Determining whether the cause of your child's defiance is situational or structural is critical to deciding the appropriate response. If there has been a situational change, you need to be understanding about what your child is going through and help him deal with the change. Revamping the way you discipline your child is not the answer. If the cause is structural, then you should address the aspects of the child's personality, or the deficits in his cognitive and social skills that underlie the child's defiance. And remember sometimes it is not your child's personality that is the issue, but rather your personality or that of your spouse. Often the solution is not to change your approach to discipline, but rather it involves addressing the underlying structural problem in your child or in yourself. If you do not figure out the right cause, you may well apply the wrong strategy.

Chart #2.1: Questions Which Will Help You Determine the Cause of Your Child's Defiance

I. **First determine whether the problem is situational or structural:**

   A.   When did your child's defiance start to become a problem?

   B.   If the defiant behavior began in the last few months, ask yourself what changed in your child's life a few months ago? (More on this topic in chapter three)

II. **If the problem has been going on for a year or more, determine whether the cause is in the child's make-up or the family structure:**

   A.   Does your child like to interact with peers? Does he have at least one good friend?

   (More on this topic in chapter four)

   B.   Is your child in danger of failing one or more of his classes?

   (Also addressed in chapter four)

   C.   Are there particular issues that your child is headstrong about, or is he defiant no matter what you ask him to do?

   (The focus of chapter five is on headstrong children, while chapter six is about children who are defiant most all the time)

   D.   How does your child behave when he is defiant? Does he lose self control and become very emotional, or is he more lawyerlike in his arguments?

   (See chapter six for types of behavioral and emotional disorders. Children who are defiant most of the time are not all the same. Some are very emotional, while others argue but do not lose their cool.)

   E.   Think about your marriage. Is there continual conflict or tension between you and your spouse?

   (Chapter seven addresses your marriage)

   F.   Does one parent have an emotional or substance abuse problem?
   (This is also discussed in chapter seven)

Chapter 3

Resolving Short Term Situational Problems

Assessment question: *You have determined that your child's defiance began in the last few months. But why did it start at this time? What has happened in your child's life that has contributed to the increase in his defiant behavior? Consider what has been happening in three major areas of your child's life: home, school, and peers.*

Look at the list of situations when your child is defiant that you charted in chapter one. Is there a theme? Are there arguments about a certain topic, like curfew, or at a certain time of day, like before school? Sometimes the issues seem petty; for example, your child has begun bothering his older siblings while they are on the phone. You need to ask yourself why is this a problem recently and not in the past? What is underlying your child's behavior? The predominant issue for many children has to do with a feeling of loss in some important relationship in the family or with peers. (It could be a real loss, like if someone dies or moves away, or something the child interprets as a loss, for example if you are preoccupied with a new job.)

Consider your child's relationships with family members and with his close friends, and think about whether anything is different. Talk with other people who know your child well. Specifically, look to see whether there has been any decrease in time your child has spent with a family member or friend. If there is a decrease, your child may feel angry about it.

On occasion, you may find that your child is actually spending *more* time with someone. If there is an increase in closeness with one of his friends, particularly if your child is a teen and has begun dating, conflicts may occur with you because your child is more interested in what his friend thinks than in what you want him to do. In this case, the cause of your teen's defiance is not a loss of time with you, but a developmental shift in your teen's relationship with you. Maturational changes are another situational cause of defiance in children, and we will explain how to handle these changes. Two maturational shifts which we will discuss in this chapter are 1) when your child reaches school age, and 2) when your child becomes an adolescent.

Your child has become defiant in the last few months, and you're wondering why. Nothing seems to have changed in your child's life. He gets along with his teacher and has some friends in school. You and your spouse love him and take him to his after school activities. At first glance, it seems like there is no reason for him to become so defiant with you. From a parent's point of view, your child's life seems stable.

I introduced you in the first two chapters to an eleven year old named Donny. He annoyed his older brother and sister by making noises while they were watching television, and he made slurping noises at dinner. These behaviors had only begun recently. Furthermore, when the parents asked Donny to stop, he argued with them and denied he had done anything wrong. He said he felt like they were picking on him and didn't trust him anymore. What seems to be the theme of Donny's behavior? Donny was trying to draw the attention of his older siblings by acting in an "obnoxious" way towards them. He was also engaging his parents in an argument, and remarked that he felt they weren't on his side. The theme of Donny's arguments with his parents was that he was feeling isolated and ignored. His behavior toward his siblings and his parents made it impossible for them to ignore him. The next question is why did Donny want to get attention at this time? Why was he feeling isolated?

You can gather more information by talking with your child and by talking with teachers and other parents. When you talk with your child, you can't usually come right out and say, "I notice you seem angry lately, what's going on?" Many children will not realize their behavior has become defiant, and they may feel you are accusing them of doing something wrong. Furthermore, even if they sense a change in their behavior, they will usually not be able to analyze why. What you want to do is ask your child about what is happening in his life without putting him "on the spot." Your focus should be on the three main areas of his life: family, school, and peers. Pick a time when you are relaxing with your child, maybe at a meal, or after a television show, or while talking before bedtime. Ask a general question like what happened in school today, or how are things with your friends? See what he says, and then ask him to tell you more about it. Your aim is to engage him in a discussion for a few minutes, so that you can assess whether there seems to be something bothering him. You should try this approach several times in the coming week, and see what your child talks about. Do any concerns emerge?

Only ask a more specific question about his mood, like "you seem upset, what is bothering you?" if your child seems in some distress at the time you speak with him. If your child is upset, and you remain non-critical and calm, you may get some very pertinent information. Your child may talk about his worries or concerns. Many times you will get only a little information, and you will need to be patient and see what your child tells you over time. Your goal is to be interested in your child and to gather information, not reach a conclusion in one discussion.

There are other sources of information which may help you figure out what is bothering your child. Check with your child's teacher, and possibly with his friends, or his friend's parents. Sometimes an outside observer will have a perspective on what is bothering your child. You could ask the other adults in your child's life if they notice whether anything is bothering your son or daughter. I would only recommend asking one of your child's peers if you yourself have a good rapport with this child and if you think your child will not be too embarrassed that you spoke with him.

You may also learn something from an unsolicited, casual remark by one of your friends. In Donny's case, one of the mother's friends remarked that she seemed so busy lately helping her older son to apply to colleges. Donny's mother remembered this remark and wondered if Donny was reacting to this change in her focus. She had been out of town visiting colleges with her older son a lot lately. And in the evenings, they were working together on his applications.

When I talked with Donny's parents about what had been changing in their lives, it became clear that both parents had become preoccupied with other issues. While the mother had been helping her older son with college applications, the father had been busier than usual at work. The parents came to recognize that they had been paying less attention to Donny over the last few months. Donny was the youngest child, and used to being a little spoiled by his parents and older siblings. He did not play after school with friends, though he got along with his peers in school. He counted on his siblings and parents to do things with him, and they were each busy with other matters.

Upon realizing the possible cause for Donny's defiance, the parents began spending more time with Donny in the evening talking about school and watching television together. They also did not respond to Donny's arguments at dinner. Essentially, they gave Donny more attention for positive behaviors, such as his efforts in school, and stopped giving Donny attention for negative behaviors, such as slurping noises at dinner. Within two months, Donny's behavior had improved dramatically. He did more of his homework, did not annoy his siblings much, and he argued less with his parents. What helped Donny was not disciplining him for his negative behavior, but understanding what he needed, and engaging him in conversation and family activities.

Chart #3.1: Determining Short Term Causes of Defiance

I. **First gather information**

    A. Use the behavior chart from chapter one and look for patterns.

    B. Talk with your child's teacher.

    C. Ask parents of your child's friends.

    D. Speak with your child in a non-confrontational way.

II. **Two kinds of situational causes**

    A. Loss of a personal connection

        1. Loss of time with one of his parents due to a schedule change

        2. Loss of time due to change in family: divorce, birth of a sibling, illness or death of a relative

        3. A good friend moving away or becoming unusually busy with an after school activity

    B. Separation issues as your child matures

        1. Separation anxiety when it is time to go to school

        2. Your teenager becomes attached to a peer(s) and is less involved in the family

Any Kind of Loss Causes Stress for Your Child

What was important in this case, as with many children under stress, is for the parents to provide what the child needs, rather than explain to the child what his problem is. The parents figured out what was underlying Donny's defiance and acted to eliminate the stressor. Donny missed spending time with his older siblings and his parents. It probably would not have helped for Donny to understand the underlying issues. Due to his age, insight about the causes of his behavior would not likely have helped Donny figure out how to get his needs met. Donny changed when his parents changed how they interacted with him. Maybe if Donny were an older teenage, he would have been able to make some changes in his behavior and reach out to his siblings and parents for support. However, even older teens may need you to change your way of relating to them before they can change.

Many of the situations that cause stress for children have to do with a loss of some kind. In Donny's case, it was everyone in his family becoming busy and paying less attention to him. No one died or moved away, but Donny felt abandoned. Adults may think that the situation is temporary and that it will not affect their children: that Dad will soon have more time, and that the older brother will soon be done applying to college. But Donny felt rejected, and it is the child's feelings which need to be understood and dealt with.

Other situations which children may experience as a loss include the birth of a sibling, moving to a new neighborhood, a grandparent's illness, a sibling's success in school or athletics, and a parent taking on new responsibilities at work or in the community. If you have to go out many evenings to visit a relative in the hospital, or if you are on some community board and have regular meetings to attend, or if you are attending a lot of your other child's athletic contests, it is possible that your child will experience this as a loss of your time and attention. Your child is more likely to feel this way if he is used to being with you most evenings or if other important people in the child's life have gotten busier at the same time.

It is also possible that your child may experience a loss in his life outside the family. If your child is older and quite attached to a particular friend, and this friend becomes rejecting, or busy with other activities, or moves away, your child may experience a feeling of loss as well. For example, it may bother him if his best friend joins the football team and cannot hang out because he has practice every day after school. While many of the changes which upset children occur in the family, some can occur in school or with peers. It is important to consider anything that that has changed in your child's life recently if there has been an increase in defiant behavior.

Why do some children become defiant when there are losses, while other children become withdrawn or sullen? There is no one answer but it probably has something to do with your child's personality and the patterns he has learned to cope with stress. Some children get angry more easily and turn to this behavior when under stress. By focusing their anger on adults and by becoming increasingly defiant with parents, children force their parents to react to them. In essence their defiant behavior makes their parents spend extra time disciplining them. The resulting interactions are negative and cause some pain for both parents and child; however, for these children some attention, even negative attention, feels better than feeling isolated. The acts of defiance have served a useful purpose for these children.

For these kinds of problems, what parents eventually want to do is help their children learn better long term coping strategies. Your child has learned that making people angry gets their attention, but in the long term, this strategy will turn people off. Your child's peers will not be as tolerant in the long term as you have been. Getting people to be empathic and listen to one's problems is a more useful long term strategy in life. Explaining this strategy to your child will probably not help much though. What will help more is having a supportive conversation with him. When your child is calmer and relaxed, try to draw him into a conversation about what is bothering him. Ask him what he thinks about a recent change in his life, such as his friend not being available, and listen if he wants to talk about it. Try to make some empathic remarks, such as "I see how that must be hard for you" or "I bet that hurts your feelings." Do not tell your child "buck up" or "come on it's not that bad." Minimizing a child's pain is usually not helpful. The child may stop telling you about his feelings, but the feelings will probably not go away.

You cannot undo all of life's pains for your child, and you cannot spend time playing with him every time he is feeling rejected. In Donny's case, fortunately the parents had the time to devote to their son, and since he was feeling rejected by them, they "undid" the rejection by talking and doing things with him. But if your child feels angry because his friends are always busy, you will probably not be able to undo his pain by playing games with him. However, spending a few minutes each day listening to what he wants to talk about will help him feel understood.

The conversations may not usually be deep or emotional. Once in a while he may share something that is bothering him, but most of the time your child is unlikely to spill his heart out to you, and may only want to talk about something non-threatening, like his progress in a video game. But asking a general question about his day and listening to his answer (even if it is about video games or other mundane topic) shows your child you care.

Remember to try to understand your child's feelings. Over time he will model this behavior with others. Because you reached out to him, your child will learn to reach out more when something is upsetting him, rather than pick a fight with someone. Sooner or later he will reach out to a new friend. Once a new friendship develops, this will help your child feel better, especially if the problem had to do with other friends being unavailable. You will likely then see a decline in defiant behavior.

Chart #3.2: Dealing with Situational Causes of Defiance

I. **If your child feels disconnected from someone important to him**

    A. Ask a general question about his day and then take time to listen to whatever your child wants to say. Your listening to him is an antidote to his feeling "cut-off."

    B. If your child does not want to talk, suggest an activity you could do together. The activity could be a game, television show, trip to the store, or cooking dinner. The key is that you do it together and that your child has an interest in the activity.

II. **If your young child does not want to leave home when it is time for school**

    A. Do not let your child engage you in a discussion about why he wants to stay home. This would likely lead to an increase in his worries or procrastination. Distraction works better. Talk about something else, or disengage by getting busy with some chore or morning activity of your own.

    B. Getting your child to school will help his fear diminish, so it is important to get him out the door pretty much on time regardless of whether he is completely ready. Remember that the goal for now is easing his separation anxiety, not having the cleanest face or teeth!

III. **If your teen argues with you about the rules**

    A. Think about the reasons for your rules and discuss the issue with your spouse first.

    B. Then discuss the issue with your teen when everyone is calm.

    C. Ask your teen if he can think of a compromise that would meet everyone's needs. Be prepared to offer a suggestion yourself if your teen does not have one.

Your Child's Development Can Bring on a Period of Defiance

As children grow, there are certain stages of development when parents and children begin to separate more from each other, and this can be a stressful time for families. One time is when children begin going to school in the primary grades. Some children do not want to leave in the mornings, and begin whining about school and may even scream when it is time to leave the house. These children may refuse to get ready in the morning, or refuse to leave the car when you arrive at school. Being defiant is one way children delay separation and express their anxiety about leaving their parents.

This can be a very trying time for parents, and many parents wonder if something is wrong at school. Usually, when parents talk with their child's teacher they find out that the child calms down after the parent leaves and that the child gets along well with staff and peers. In some cases, there may be anxiety symptoms at other times during the school day. For example, a child may miss a parent at lunch, particularly if he does not have a peer he likes to sit with. Or he may fall down at recess, and wish his mother were there to take care of him. It is important for parents not to rescue the child if he goes to the nurse because he falls down or because he feels a little sick. Your child will see that everything works out when a teacher or the nurse helps him. It does not have to be his mom or dad who takes care of him in every situation.

If your child throws a tantrum after you drop him off at school, do not linger or delay the separation as a result of the child's defiant behavior. Have the school deal with your child's tantrum, because it is likely to last much longer if you stay around. Over the coming days or weeks, your child will see that everything works out when he goes to school and will also see that he gets plenty of time with you after school. Your child will get used to the new routine and begin to feel more confident and more cooperative in the mornings before school.

Another life stage that can bring on defiant behavior is separation during adolescence. Your older child will likely begin to develop deeper attachments with friends and spend less time with you and the family. In some cases, your teenager may not agree with the rules you set about the time he can spend on the computer or the time he must come home on the weekends or evenings. He may repeatedly violate these rules, and it is also possible his defiance will spread to other peer-related issues, like hair style, piercings, type of clothes, or even experimentation with alcohol. If your child has not been defiant before and now begins to challenge a number of your rules, then it is likely that a relationship with one or more peers has become very important to him. Being with the peers and pleasing them has taken precedence over pleasing you.

This is what is happening to Felicia, a teenager I introduced you to earlier in the book. She still cared about her mother, but wanted to spend more time with her boyfriend, even if this was against her mother's wishes. Felicia was beginning to separate from her mother and get closer to her friends, especially her boyfriend. She had begun lying about where she was going so that she could see the boyfriend more than her mother wanted. The mother found this out one day when she followed Felicia after Felicia left the house. Felicia had said she was going to see her girlfriends, but what happened was that one of her girlfriends picked her up and dropped her off at the boyfriend's house. The mother was fuming, went home, and called her daughter's cell phone. She told Felicia to come home immediately. The daughter returned, and there was a loud confrontation followed by the daughter running up to her room and sobbing for half an hour. What should this mother do?

When I spoke with the mother later about that day, I explained that her daughter's wishes to be with her boyfriend were age appropriate, but the mother felt her daughter was being rash. The mother feared Felicia would go too far sexually and get pregnant. Many teens do engage in sexual behavior: slightly less than half of high school students have had intercourse, according to recent statistics. I suggested the mother talk with her daughter about her concerns about pregnancy and also about sexually transmitted diseases. I also urged her to have her daughter see a gynecologist to talk about these issues. Talking does not mean encouraging her to have sex. It means being mindful of the statistics and doing what you can to make sure your daughter is safe if she chooses to have sex.

I know this is a controversial subject for many parents and their teens. Felicia was in her junior year in high school, and in eighteen months she would be going to college. The mother would not have a lot of control then for sure. Furthermore, Felicia did not have a history of being rash and impulsive. The alternative to leaving some of these decisions up to Felicia was to try to stop her from being alone with the boyfriend. However, the boyfriend's parents were not willing to help, and if the mother tried to prevent Felicia from seeing him, she would probably see him behind her back. It seemed that the most prudent thing for the mother to do was to put all the cards on the table and to tell Felicia her concerns.

The mother reported back to me after she had a heart to heart conversation with her daughter. The daughter said she loved her boyfriend, but was not having intercourse and was not planning to do so. The mother hoped this was the case. However, I explained to the mother that it was possible her daughter was not telling her everything since most teens do not discuss the details of their sexual activities with their parents. As I suggested, the mother made an appointment with the gynecologist so that her daughter could ask whatever questions she wanted in private with her doctor. The mother and daughter also talked over how often she would see her boyfriend and when she would spend time at home, e.g. for family dinners and studying weeknights for school. They reached a compromise, which held for the rest of the school year. They would talk again about what to do during the summer when the time came.

In general, if your teen does not want to follow many of your rules, you will probably want to set some limits, but compromise on those rules that are less critical to you. You should work as a team with your spouse if possible. Where you draw the line will depend in part on your values and in part on your child's maturity. Sometimes talking with your teen when everyone is calm helps both you and her to see each other's concerns. Sometimes it is difficult to compromise. Ultimately, parents must decide what the rules will be, but try to take into account your child's friendship needs and think about a safe way for her to meet those needs.

I advise parents to be more lenient on issues that are not a matter of health and safety. For example, I recommend that parents not make a big issue out of clothes or hair style. Instead, you should focus on issues like alcohol experimentation and repeated curfew violations. Sexual behavior carries risks as well, and when you feel your teen may become sexually active, you should have a frank talk about the emotional and biological implications. Parents often do not know exactly when their teen becomes sexually active, so it is better to have some discussions sooner rather than later.

Sometimes defiance is even more extreme during adolescence. For example, some teens argue with their parents about anything they are asked to do around the house. Or, if parents limit their teen's activities in some way, for example, if they ask their child to be home early on Sunday for a family dinner, an argument may ensue and quickly get out of hand. Some teenagers go so far as to leave the house when they are angry and stay out at a friend's over night without permission. There are other worrisome signs of defiance which may appear during the teen years. Some teens will hang out with their friends at a coffee shop before school and show up late to their first class. Others will begin to argue with teachers. Usually in these more extreme cases, there have been signs of defiant behavior even earlier in a child's life. Defiance may escalate in adolescence due to developmental factors, but the underlying pattern of behavior has existed for years. A repeated pattern of defiance over years is the subject of the next three chapters which focus on long term, structural causes.

What To Do and What Not To Do

For children who feel less connected with you or someone else:

1. Don't tell your child it's not such a big deal and he should get over it.

2. Don't buy things for him to feel better.

3. Don't exempt him from his usual responsibilities.

4. Don't punish his defiant behavior, unless he is physically aggressive, i.e. he pushes or hits someone. Since these children are being defiant to get attention, it is generally not necessary to use punishments, and sometimes punishment makes them feel more alienated from adults.

5. Ignore the defiant behavior, and later when your child is not being defiant, try to engage him in a conversation or activity. Show your child that people are more likely to respond to him when he is calm than when he is disagreeable.

6. Brief activities for fifteen to thirty minutes on a regular basis (several times a week) are better than an infrequent (once a month) outing.

7. Don't expect to have deep conversations with your child about his feelings. Try to engage him in a conversation about his day. If he mentions a problem, make a brief statement that shows you understood what happened, and then see if your child goes on to say anything else about his feelings. If he does, listen and be empathic. If he does not have much to say, you could a) talk about something that happened that day in your life, or b) ask about something else your child did at school or at home that day, or c) begin an activity together.

For young children who become defiant when it is time for school:

1.   Don't ask your child how he feels about going to school. The more you focus on the upcoming separation, the more anxious and defiant your child will become.

2.   Use distraction if your child is fretful or disagreeable. Talk about something else happening that day, or ask about how your child liked something he did yesterday.

3.   Be cheerful yourself, and do not act worried that your child will be sad or have a tantrum. Anxiety can be contagious.

4.   If on a regular basis your child is defiant or tantrums when you are helping him get ready for school, then have another adult take your place, if possible, while you do something else.

5.   Keep the time of separation as brief as possible. Do not linger when your child leaves you. The longer the separation period the harder it will be for you and for your child.

6.   If your child has a tantrum at school, you should leave and let the school deal with it. Your child will calm down sooner if you are not around.

7.   Don't visit your child a lot at school while your child is having problems with separation. Also, if your child has anxiety symptoms at school (like stomach aches) and if the school nurse calls you, do not get on the phone with your child. If your child's separation problems lead to more interaction with you, then the problems are likely to get worse.

8.   Expect to have an increase in defiant behavior after school vacations or, in some cases, after weekends. Once your child is used to staying home on his days off, it may be hard to start back to school.

9.   When you see your child after school, talk about what your child learned or did at school that was positive, rather than about any anxiety symptoms. If your child brings up an anxiety symptom, listen but then change the subject to what happened in school that was fun or interesting.

10. If you are having difficulty getting your child to school on time, don't allow your child to stay home. Going to school for even part of a day is important because it allows your child to

see that he can separate from you and that nothing terrible happens. Children sometimes express the fear that some harm will come to you or to them while they are out of your sight. Only when they go to school and see with their own eyes that nothing horrible happens will their anxiety lessen.

For teens who begin to defy your rules:

1. Think first before you react: a) what lies behind your child's recent defiance? What does he really want? b) What do you really want, and what are you willing to give up control over?

2. Sit with your teen and explain what you see as the dilemma when everyone is calm. Say that you will take a break if the discussion gets heated, and do that if an argument ensues.

3. Talk about the pros and cons of letting your child do what he wants, rather than paint your feelings as right and your child's feelings as wrong. Don't put down your child.

4. Compromise on issues that are not paramount to your child's health and safety. Then see if your child sticks to the agreement. Does your child do what he said he would? Does anything go wrong if you let him have more freedom? If things work out, continue with the new plan. If not, suspend the agreement for a period of time (a week for relatively minor infractions such as coming home late without calling you ahead of time) and then try again.

5. If your teen shows he can be responsible, be prepared to continue to compromise with him. Remember that the goal of this stage of development is to have your teen become more and more independent.

6. If your teen continually breaks agreements, consider whether there are additional issues besides your teen wanting to be more independent. Read the rest of this book to see if there could be other causes and other solutions!

7. Talk with the parents of your child's friends, especially if you know them and trust them. See if you and the other parents can come up with similar rules about curfew and about what activities are permissible. Your child will be less defiant if his friends have similar rules.

Chapter 4

Serious Academic or Social Problems

Assessment questions:

1. Does your child like to interact with peers and have at least one good friend?

2. Is your child in danger of failing one or more of his classes?

If your answer to question one is no, then there is the possibility that your child has a problem interacting with other people, and you should read the section below on autistic spectrum disorders. If your answer is yes, then move on to question 2.

If your child is in danger of failing one or more classes, then there is the possibility that your child has a learning disability. You should read the second section of this chapter which is about learning disabilities.

Either learning problems or social interaction problems can be stressful for your child and can underlie his defiance toward adults. Unless these issues are dealt with, your child's defiance is unlikely to change. In this chapter we will consider what to do if your child is doing poorly in school or has no friends. If your child's school work is average or better, and if he has one or more friends, then you can skip to the next chapter.

Autistic Spectrum Disorders

If your child has no friends, there is the possibility that the child has an autistic spectrum disorder. You will need to determine if this is the case, or if your child is just shy. Shy children enjoy interacting with other children once a connection with someone is established. They have trouble approaching peers, and usually wait for others to show interest in them. When a friendship is established, they look forward to meeting with their friend, and miss the friend when he is not around. It is different for most autistic children, who prefer to play alone and who often have trouble engaging in a back and forth conversation with peers.

Autism is generally thought of as a continuum of disorders; hence the term autistic spectrum disorders (ASD). The most severe disability is actually labeled "autism," less severe is "Asperger's disorder", and least severe is "pervasive developmental disorder, not otherwise specified" (PDD-NOS). In this chapter, I will focus mostly on children with Asperger's or PDD-NOS. These terms come from the diagnostic manual used by most mental health professionals. The manual is called *Diagnostic and Statistical Manual-Fourth Edition* (DSM-IV). The key characteristics of all three forms of ASD are 1) social interaction difficulties and 2) preoccupation with a limited number of interests or activities. Children with these disorders have trouble bonding with others and prefer solitary play. There is usually not the sharing of ideas and feelings that can be seen in more normal childhood friendships.

The most severe form of ASD is known as autistic disorder. Children with autistic disorder not only have trouble interacting with others, but have limited spoken language skills. It is also difficult to get these children to look at you when it is necessary to communicate something to them. Some of these children do not develop speech, and can only be taught basic gestures to express what they want. Other autistic children learn words to express themselves, but may not express a complete thought when they are speaking with you. Sometimes autistic children repeat certain phrases many times during the day, such as their favorite jingles from television shows or movies.

Autistic children have very rigid interests, and often want to play a favorite activity or watch the same movie over and over again. For example, some autistic children are fascinated by cars or trains and will play with a toy train on and off for hours. The particular interest varies with the child, but it is often a machine or animal, not a social activity, like a sport. Since most of their peers are more interested in sports than trains, it is difficult for these children to find an interest in common with their peers.

A more communicative form of ASD is known as Asperger's disorder. These children do not generally have trouble learning how to speak when they are two and three years old, like autistic children do. However, children with Asperger's still do have difficulty relating to other people and still have fairly rigid and limited interests. Asperger's children do not usually approach peers to engage in an activity and when asked to join in, they are reluctant to do so, unless it is one of their favorite activities. For example, one area of interest for some Asperger's children which can be shared with other children is Japanese trading cards, such as Yugio or Pokemon cards. These cards are very detailed and playing with them does not require much social interaction. If the conversation switches to another topic, Asperger's children will usually withdraw and play by themselves. There is not the flexibility to try new activities or to engage in conversations about new topics.

The third form of ASD that some children exhibit is called pervasive developmental disorder, not otherwise specified (PDD-NOS). These children have some difficulty interacting with other people and exhibit some rigidity in their interests, but many of these children will play and talk with a peer, if the peer does not put too much pressure on the PDD-NOS child to try a lot of new activities or to join a larger group which might be uncomfortable for the PDD child. For example, if the peer is interested in playing a video game which your PDD-NOS child also enjoys, they may hit it off and get together after school. But if the friend also wants to play baseball in the neighborhood, which your child may not enjoy, then the friendship will be limited. Often as PDD-NOS children reach adolescence it gets harder for them to sustain meaningful friendships because many of their peers begin dating and go to parties or larger social gatherings on the weekends. These activities often make PDD-NOS teens feel uncomfortable. (Notice that the diagnoses of Asperger's and PDD-NOS overlap. Some mental health professionals use PDD-NOS for those ASD children who have more social skills, while other mental health professionals do not use the PDD-NOS label, and instead refer to these children as being at the high end of Asperger's.)

Chart # 4.1: Characteristics of Autistic Spectrum Disorders and Learning Disabilities

I.   **Autistic spectrum disorders**

    A.   Autistic disorder

        1.   Difficulty with social interaction as evidenced by disinterest in peer relationships, a lack of sharing ideas and interests with others, and an impairment in nonverbal communication skills, such as a failure to make eye contact when speaking with someone

        2.   Difficulty with communication, such as an inability to use spoken language, or a marked impairment in social language (for example, repeating certain words and phrases over and over)

        3.   Preoccupation with only a few interests or activities (preferring to do the same activity over and over again) and sometimes unusual and repetitive motor behaviors (for example, hand or finger flapping)

    B.   Asperger's disorder

        1.   Problems with social interaction and a preoccupation with a limited number of activities, similar to characteristics #1 and #3 of autistic disorder

        2.   Basic language skills developed normally. (#2 above for Autistic Disorder does not apply to Asperger's Disorder.) However, there are often subtle communication problems, such as not knowing how to enter a conversation appropriately, not perceiving nuance, and misunderstanding non-literal speech.

    C.   Pervasive developmental disorder not otherwise specified (PDD-NOS)

        1.   There is some avoidance of social interaction, particularly in large group settings. However, these children have peer relationships in which there is some sharing of ideas and interests, more than for autistic or Asperger's children.

    2.   Preoccupation with a few interests or activities, but more flexibility than seen with autistic and Asperger's children

II. Learning disabilities

A.   Significant variation in a person's cognitive abilities, such that there is a weakness in one or more skills that is affecting the student's performance in school.

B.   Overall intellectual level is at age level or above.

Strategies for Defiance in ASD Children

Children with autistic spectrum disorder often exhibit some defiant behavior toward their parents, and the underlying issue is often the children's very narrow interests. Typically, family life consists of a variety of activities, some of which may not be fun or interesting to ASD children. If an activity or family outing falls outside the child's range of interests, he can become very resistant and sometimes verbally defiant. In addition, everyday activities, like meal times or bedtime can be a struggle because the ASD child gets busy with his own preferred activity and does not want to put down what he is doing. The rigidity of these children gets in the way, and it is the rigidity which must be the target of any intervention you undertake, if you want to have smoother interactions, with less acting out.

Think about how you can motivate your ASD child to compromise, to be more flexible. Do not focus on the hostile words your child may utter when you insist that he put away his favorite toys and prepare for a different activity, such as reading, or showering before bed. Your child's hostile words are a sign of his inflexibility, and if you can figure out a way to "by-pass" your child's inflexibility, there will be no hostilities! One option is to plan ahead and try to have your child participate in the less preferred activity *before* he plays with his toys. That way you do not have to interrupt his play time. For example, if you know your child does not like reading, you should have him do that first, and allow him to play with his toys afterward. If your child does not stay focused on his book and begins to daydream instead, you could remind him once or twice that if he finishes reading, he can play with his toys. Use this strategy on any day that you want your child to read. In a sense you are beginning a new routine for your child: read, then play.

Another suggestion is to think about what is essential for your child to do in a given day, and what you can let go. It will be difficult to motivate your ASD child to do everything you might want, so think about what is more important: maybe doing homework is more important than taking out the dog, for example. It is up to you to decide where you want to put your energy.

Once you decide what is important to you, think about which activities are important to your child. You can use these activities as rewards when your child shows some flexibility. If he can stop what he is doing and pay attention to one of your requests, you can reward him by offering to join him in some special activity of his choosing. Remember that the activity he chooses does not begin until after he has finished doing what you requested. This sequence of activities (such that your child's favorite activity comes second) is similar to the suggestion I made above for the child who does not like to read. The only difference is that this time the preferred activity is called a "reward" and includes you. You engage in the preferred activity with your child. For example, for children who like Japanese trading cards, they could earn fifteen or twenty minutes to play Pokemon with you if they take a shower on time. (Of course this means you have to be willing to play Pokemon; if you cannot stand this game, try to find another activity that you both like!) The reward has the added advantage of being a social activity, because your child will be interacting with you when the game is played. In this way, you are also helping him practice for interactions that he will have someday with peers.

Sometimes there is not time on a school day to earn a special activity with you. In this case, try awarding "flexibility" points if your child can adjust to what you request. Then he can trade in the points on certain days to do a special activity with you. We call these points "flexibility" points to emphasize to your child that the goal is to be flexible. Another label I sometimes use is "go with the flow" points. It's the same idea, but a more colloquial phrase. In order for this to work, you should not ask too often for your child to earn these points each day, because it will be hard for your child to adapt his interests to the family's schedule throughout the day. Give your child the opportunity to earn these points once or twice a day, and make sure that the special activity he could earn is really what your child wants to do. If your child does not care about the activity that much, or if he gets to do the activity sometimes regardless of his points, then it is less likely that the "flexibility" points will motivate him.

Let's revisit one of the children I introduced in the first chapter: Arthur. He would not listen to his parents' requests to come to dinner, to do his homework, or to take a shower and get ready for bed. Also, once the parents got him to take a shower in the evening, he would stay in the bathroom for a very long time. Sometimes he got quite angry with his parents when they insisted he listen to their directions. Once, Arthur even told his father "I hope you die." The common denominator for the conflicts with Arthur was that his parents asked him to switch from an activity of his choosing to an activity of their choosing. No matter what the parents asked him to do, Arthur was insistent about continuing whatever he was doing. Arthur suffered from Asperger's. He had no friends and was interested primarily in reading gardening magazines and decorating the house with holiday or seasonal ornaments. He also enjoyed reading some science fiction books and watching a couple of television shows.

With this child, the parents were encouraged to think about developing a new routine so that what Arthur wanted to do would come after one or more of his responsibilities. For example, he could not watch his favorite television program until his homework was done. Furthermore, he earned "decorating" time if he cooperated with dinner and bedtime routines.

These strategies helped, but did not always work. Sometimes Arthur was "in his own world" and no incentive mattered to him. Reminders about what he needed to do in order to earn an incentive did not help. Sometimes Arthur also made rude comments to his mother or father. At these times, the parents were instructed to ignore his arguments and rude remarks. For example, if it was getting late in the evening and Arthur had not finished his homework, Arthur would argue that he could not go to bed until he completed his work. Parents learned to ignore Arthur's arguments and to insist on the lights being out at a certain time. There would be a consequence at school, such as a poor grade or a detention, if Arthur did not complete his homework. Sometimes it is helpful if parents do not worry too much about their child's homework, but rather take a deep breath, and let the "natural" consequences at school occur. Arthur cared about his grades and did not want to get a lot of zeros. In time, the natural consequence of receiving lower grades motivated Arthur to finish his homework before bedtime. The parents could have yelled or made threats to get Arthur's attention, but then Arthur would have become increasingly hostile and probably would not have gotten much more of his homework done anyway.

You will not always be able to reach an autistic child. Sometimes if you are having trouble motivating your child, try varying the incentives because your child's interests may be changing. He may become bored with the same incentive after a while. Occasionally taking away a privilege may be necessary to make your point; however, excessive punishment is not useful. Autistic children are likely to withdraw into their own thoughts if parents are too punitive. At times, parents need to take a break and wait a half hour, or longer, to see if the child becomes more reachable later. There can be a fluctuation in an autistic child's attentiveness to the parents from hour to hour and from day to day. Hang in there because tomorrow may be better!

I want to make one more suggestion at this point about helping ASD children, and, if you are interested in learning even more about ASD, you can read one of the ASD books recommended in chapter ten. Since one of the primary difficulties for these children has to do with social skills, consider whether your child's school or community offers structured settings for practicing social interaction. Ideally, your child could meet with other ASD children in a group at school where they could talk and get to know each other. The students could be encouraged by the adult leader, a school counselor or social worker, to develop their social skills, such as calling someone on the phone to come over and play after school. First, the students would role play making phone calls, and then after school try to call one of the other group members on the phone. They would report back about their "social" homework the next time the group met. This kind of group is called a social skills training group.

You can also enroll your child in an after school or community activity with peers, such as scouts, an exercise class, an art program, or some other class of interest. The key is to pick an activity where your child can sometimes work independently on an interest of his, and also begin to interact with peers who have a similar interest. Do not pick activities that require a high level of peer interaction, such as a team sport, unless your child has excellent athletic skills and can handle the repartee that occurs between teammates. There are many benefits to your child to participating in some kind of activity group. He will become more proficient in the activity, which helps his self-esteem, and at the same time he gets practice in communicating and in sharing. Group activities also help ASD children develop greater flexibility. The more your child experiences social situations that call for some give and take, the better the chances your child will become more flexible. Someday your child may be able to shift gears more easily when you need him to do something at home!

Chart #4.2: How To Help ASD or LD Children

I.   Helping with the inflexibility of ASD children:

    A.   Structure the day so that what he wants to do comes after what you want him to do.

    B.   Have your child earn "flexibility" or "go with the flow" points when you ask him to stop what he is doing and switch to what you need him to do. These points can be redeemed for activities your child prefers.

    C.   If incentives do not work, sometimes it helps if you ignore your child's negative behavior and let natural consequences occur. This only works though if your child cares about the natural consequences.

    D.   Do not focus on changing too many behaviors at once. Pick your spots.

II.   Helping ease the frustration for LD children:

    A.   Explain to your child why a subject is hard for him.

    B.   Arrange help in school and/or after school so that the disability does not hinder your child's learning as much.

    C.   Be sensitive about the disability during homework time and offer help on harder items.

Learning Disabilities

If your child is receiving many low grades in some of his classes, it could be because your child has a learning disability. If this is the case, you might see more frustration and also greater defiance when it is time to do homework. The work is so difficult that it engenders feelings of unhappiness and feelings of failure, which may lead to acting out by your child. You may see signs of irritability and defiance even when there is no homework because your child might be feeling weighed down by the stress of the work he had in school.

What is a learning disability? Basically, it occurs when there is significant unevenness in a person's intellectual capabilities. We all have some strengths and weaknesses in our cognitive abilities; however, for a person with a learning disability, there is a more significant weakness in some skill(s). Overall, people with a learning disability have about average intellectual skills, and sometimes above average skills. However, there are some area(s) that are significantly below their other abilities.

A person with a learning disability may have trouble in one or more subjects in school. For example, a child may not do well in math or reading. In order to know what to do for this child, it is important to figure out why this is happening. School psychologists and learning specialists are trained to figure out why a child is having trouble; in other words, what is the underlying cognitive process that is causing the trouble in math or reading? If the child has trouble learning multiplication for example, is the problem due to a lack of attention, or is it due to memory issues, or does the child have trouble understanding the concept of multiplication?

Let's take each of these three possible causes in turn: attention, memory, and conceptual thinking. One important underlying cognitive skill is attention. In order to learn, children must be able to focus on what the teacher is explaining. If a child gets distracted by other sounds in the classroom or by other ideas going through his head and cannot focus on what the teacher is saying, then that child will have trouble in school. The child may have the ability to do the work when he listens, but because he is distracted so much, the child does not do well in school. These children may be diagnosed with attention deficit hyperactivity disorder (see chapter six for the criteria for ADHD), but there can be other causes of difficulty with attention, such as problems with auditory processing. I refer you in chapter ten to other books where you can learn more about these problems.

Another type of learning problem is difficulty with memory. There are different kinds of memory: one is immediate memory, which has to do with the ability to keep information in mind and to be able to work on it mentally before giving an answer. For example, if your child has to solve a math problem in his head, he has to keep all the facts in his brain while he then manipulates the numbers in order to reach the correct answer. He may know how to do the mathematical operation, but may forget one of the numbers, and therefore get the wrong answer. If he wrote down the problem, he might get the right answer because there would be less pressure on his memory. For this child, it might seem there is a weakness in math, but the underlying problem may have to do with memory.

Another kind of memory problem is long term memory. When a child is reading a book and comes upon an unusual word that he may have learned a few months ago, if his long term memory is weak, he will have difficulty remembering what the word means. He may then miss the meaning of the sentence, and get the wrong answer on a test question. However, if the teacher had given him the definition of the word, he might have understood better what he was reading and gotten the right answer. Reading problems can be caused by many different factors, and one of them is long term recall of the meaning of words.

Another important mental skill necessary for reading is called decoding. When a child reads a word that is unfamiliar, he needs to sound it out. If he does not know how to break down a word into parts or does not know how the different parts sound, then he will have difficulty figuring out the word. This will make reading frustrating. Decoding is a critical skill in the primary grades when children are learning to read.

A problem with reading or math can be caused by other factors. Another possibility is difficulty understanding abstract concepts. Does a child understand what multiplication is all about? If a child does not understand the concept behind what he is doing, it will be harder to learn. For the concept of multiplication, a teacher can help make the learning process more real for the child by using concrete objects, like coins or marbles, and showing the child what happens when you multiply two sets of objects.

These are a few of the kinds of learning problems children can have. The first sign of a disability is often that a child is struggling with one or more subjects in school, even though he seems capable in other ways, either in school or outside school. For example, he may be great at chess, fixing the computer, or with numbers, but struggle in English class. If your child is doing poorly in some subjects, then you can request a learning evaluation to determine if your child has an underlying disability. A learning specialist or psychologist will give your child a variety of tests in order to figure out what the underlying problem is.

Before asking for a learning evaluation, I would suggest that you talk with your child's teachers to see what they think is going on with your child. There can be many reasons why a child is not learning in school, and a learning disability is just one of the possible causes. Many children do not do well in school because of emotional problems or because of motivational issues. If your child is unhappy or anxious, then he may not pay attention well in school and will have trouble with his work. Or your child may not think that doing well in school is as important as making friends, and may be focused on impressing his peers rather than focused on listening to a lecture by one of his teachers. See what your child's teacher is observing in the class. Compare what she says with what your child says about school and with what you observe when your child is doing homework. Is there a common theme to what everyone thinks is happening? If there is the possibility of a learning disability, then ask for an evaluation by a specialist. If there is no consensus about the possible cause, it is still worth asking the school to look further into the problem. Sometimes, what seems at times to be a lack of interest in a subject is really caused by an inability to understand the material. Your child may act unmotivated but really be struggling to learn and not want to admit it.

In most school districts, parents can request a case study evaluation if a child is performing poorly. The case study evaluation will include testing to help determine whether your child has a learning disability. Schools are required by law to figure out how to help your child learn.

After the evaluation is complete, you will be invited to meet with the teacher and other staff to talk about the results and what to do. If your child does *not* have a disability, and if the problem is due to motivational or emotional factors, then I will address what you should do in the following chapters about personality and family issues. If your child has a disability, your child will be offered extra services, such as small group, or one-on-one, instruction in the area of his disability. You may also want to get additional help after school by hiring an educational therapist. Educational therapists are specially trained to help children with learning disabilities.

Learning Disabilities and Defiance

Once your child feels hopeful that he can improve, he will likely feel less unhappy and less defiant. You should explain to your child that the interventions planned in school will help him, and encourage him to let you know how it is going. If he feels a part of the process, he will likely feel more involved, more hopeful, and more energized. This change in behavior may not occur right after the determination of a learning disability is made, however. Many children will not feel better until they feel some success in school. Once children see that the extra help is working, they will likely be less frustrated and less defiant.

In the first chapter, one of the children I introduced to you had a learning disability. Her name was Ginny. One of the primary times she was defiant with her parents was at homework time. She would refuse to do her homework and tell her parents to leave her alone. If they insisted, she got louder and sometimes had a tantrum. If she did sit down to do her homework, her parents needed to be close by, or Ginny would give up and leave many parts undone.

Ginny's problem was with reading, and more specifically she had difficulty decoding words. She could not easily break a new word down into its parts and sound it out. A reading problem will have a major effect on a child's success in school. Any written work will be difficult if a child has trouble reading. It was no wonder that Ginny struggled with her homework and tried to avoid it. Once Ginny began getting extra help at school, the struggles at home lessened. She still resisted at times, but the level of defiance was significantly reduced.

When doing homework with a child with learning disabilities, try to determine what she is capable of and give her a hand with more difficult items. In Ginny's case, the parents helped her read her assignments. They did *not* make her sound out most of the words she could not figure out, but instead said them out loud for her. It would have been too frustrating and would have taken too long if they had asked Ginny to attempt to read every word of her homework herself. The parents were lenient in other ways as well. If some of Ginny's written answers were wrong, the parents were still positive afterward about her efforts and did not ask her to redo many items. Remember that this is a sensitive issue for your child, and she does not want to feel like a failure, especially in front of her parents.

Sometimes, it helps to have a homework tutor, or preferably an educational therapist (who is trained to help children with learning disabilities), if your child is especially sensitive about making mistakes in front of you or your spouse. An educational therapist can not only help your child with her homework, but also help your child learn to overcome her disability. Sometimes it is difficult to afford a tutor or educational therapist on a regular basis. In that case, rather than always do the homework with you, your child may be more relaxed working with an older sibling or grandparent. Think about what works for your child. You will probably find there are fewer problems at home if she is feeling less stress about her work.

In general, defiant behaviors will lessen if your child feels competent rather than like a failure. If teachers or parents push too hard, or focus too much on a child's problems, it is very possible your child will feel "stupid." When there is a loss of self-esteem, many children will become more irritable with their parents. What is even more humiliating for most children than looking "stupid" in front of their parents or teachers is if an adult exposes a child's weakness to his peers; for example, some children are horrified if a teacher inadvertently exposes their weakness in front of the whole class. If that happens, some children become quiet and withdrawn while others become angry and defiant. It all depends on a child's way of dealing with stress. To prevent these bad outcomes, it is important that all the adults working with your child be sensitive to things that can hurt his self-esteem.

In this chapter we have focused on your child's school performance and peer relationships in order to determine if there is a learning disability or autistic spectrum disorder. These issues are not the most common cause of defiance, but they need to be ruled out because the approach is very different than what I will recommend for other problems that can bring on defiant behavior. The next chapter will help you figure out what to do if there are other causes of your child's defiance. We will look at personality features that can bring on defiant behavior.

What To Do and What Not To Do

For ASD children:

1. Do not despair if your child does not improve right away. As your child gets older, you will likely begin to notice some ways in which he is more flexible. It's a gradual process.

2. Think about what's really important. What do you really need your child to pay attention to? For less important matters, if your child is self-absorbed and does not respond to you, let it go.

3.   If you need your child to do something, but he is focused on another activity or on his own thoughts, decide if you need him to pay attention to you right away. If you do not need him to do something right away, sometimes your child will be more amenable to listening to you after he finishes with what he is doing. However, sometimes what he is doing can drag on for hours!

4.   If you do need his attention right away, stand near him and speak in a calm but firm manner. If he does not seem to hear you, ask him to look at you. Stay calm and repeat yourself. Keep your sentences brief and to the point. Focus on *what* you need your child to do. You do not need to explain *why* you need his cooperation.

5.   Be prepared to stay there until your child begins to comply with your request. Do not give him a time limit to do what you request and then walk away. It works better to be insistent that your child cooperate while you are present to make sure he is fully attending to your request.

6.   Consequences usually are not effective unless you find something your child really cares about. The same is true for incentives. Think about what your child really likes to do, even if you feel the activity is childish or peculiar. The problem is that many ASD children enjoy their private thoughts so much that usual rewards and consequences which you might impose, such as phone or television privileges, may not carry much weight with them.

7.   Sometimes speaking in a silly, or funny, way gets your child's attention. Your tone is different than the way you usually speak. Your child may laugh or giggle, but the point is that your child hears you and is more likely to cooperate. You will still need to stand there to make sure your child does not return to his own activity.

8.   Do not take away a social activity if your child is not cooperative with you. ASD children need to participate in social situations in order to grow, so that this kind of consequence would have a negative effect on your child.

9.   Try to think of social activities in your school or community that your child might enjoy. For example, if he is interested in

Japanese trading cards, ask other parents if they know of a place where children get together to play these games. The focus of the activity is less important than the fact that it involves interacting with other people.

10. It is likely that your child's grades in school will be somewhat uneven. There may be a significant drop off in his effort when the subject matter does not interest him. Don't get angry with your child. Ask yourself whether it will really matter in the long run if your child does not get a good grade in some class. Also, speak with the teachers to let them know of your child's interests. (Maybe the teacher can give your child an assignment that fits better with his interests—for example, if your child is interested in snakes maybe he can write a report on a book about snakes.) When your child is in high school and there are electives, enroll him in classes that hold more interest for him.

For LD Children:

1. If your child is teased by peers or his siblings for being "stupid" or "having a disability", let your child know everyone has strengths and weaknesses in life. Give him an example of his strengths. Reassure him that a learning weakness does not at all mean that he is "stupid."

2. Admire something your child does well (preferably at the time he does it so that he sees what you are referring to). You can admire something he does at home, in school, or with his peers.

3. Sign your child up for an activity after school that he enjoys.

4. There's a fine line between encouraging your child to persevere in the area of his disability and pushing your child too hard. During homework time, listen for signs your child is getting too frustrated and suggest he take a break. You can suggest he return to the work later when his frustration eases, but sometimes settle for him completing some of the work correctly, rather than all of it. How much you push depends on your child's frustration level and on how hard the homework is. If you are unsure, speak with teachers or other parents who have experience with LD issues.

5.   If your child gets emotional on a regular basis when you are helping him with his homework, think about having some other adult work with your child instead. Some children do not want to make mistakes in front of their parents.

6.   Help your child keep school in perspective. There are several possible ways to do this. One way is to talk regularly about other activities he enjoys. Another is to point out that for much of his life he will *not* be in school and that when he is an adult he will be able choose a job that he is good at. You could also explain that when he is an adult no one will ask him if he has a learning disability.

7.   Here's another way to show him that people with learning disabilities do well in life: You and your child could go online (or go to the library) and find out about famous people who were successful despite having learning disabilities.

Chapter 5

Approaches for Headstrong Children

Assessment question: *You have determined that your child's defiant behavior has been going on for a long time. Is there a particular issue(s) that your child is defiant about, or is he defiant no matter what you ask him to do? If he is defiant with you only some of the time, then your child may have a strong-willed personality.*

Go back over the list of situations when your child is defiant that you created when reading chapter one. How often do these confrontations occur? Is there a particular issue(s) about which your child argues, or is he defiant no matter what you ask him to do? And how long does the defiant behavior usually last? If your child's defiance 1) usually lasts for less than a half hour and 2) does not occur with many of the things you ask of him, then it is more likely that your child is strong-willed, but does not have a psychological disorder. There are strategies you can use for strong willed children, which we will cover in this chapter.

Some strong-willed children have a secondary problem, which I call "anger overload." This means they have difficulty calming down when they get angry. In the latter section of this chapter, I will explain what you should do if your strong willed child experiences anger overload.

If your child is defiant for most things you want him to do, or if the struggles go on for an hour or more several times a week, it is more likely that your child has a psychological problem that needs to be dealt with. In that case, you will want to pay particular attention to chapter six, the chapter after this one.

Strong-willed Children Who Are Disagreeable Only Sometimes

When it comes to following adult rules, strong-willed children are sometimes quite defiant. Strong-willed children have some specific ideas and preferences, and they do not like to defer to other people on subjects about which they feel passionately. If a parent's request touches on one of these issues, the strong-willed child will not give in easily, and may erupt into a tirade. What's interesting is that these children are not always uncompromising. It depends upon whether something they value strongly is at stake. They do not look for conflict, but they will not shy away from it when they care about something. If you do not know how to handle it, you and your child can have some loud and unpleasant struggles!

Strong-willed children also tend to tell their peers what to do, and conflicts can arise if the peers do not go along. Strong-willed children usually have certain preferences when it comes to play, and they like to set the agenda. They tend to seek out peers who are more passive and agreeable. If they come up against another strong-willed child, sometimes there will be a conflict, and then one of the children may walk away in a huff.

I don't want you to think that being strong-willed will only bring your child trouble! The benefit of being strong-willed is that these children are likely to pursue their goals in life even when facing potential roadblocks. Their determination can be an asset. But in order to avoid regular conflict with others, they also need to learn to compromise at times. If your strong-willed child can learn how to balance his determination to meet his goals with an ability to cooperate with others, you and your child will suffer less heartache along the way! This chapter will outline some ideas to help you teach your strong-willed child to cooperate better with others.

Chart #5.1: Characteristics of Headstrong Children

I.   Children are strong-willed and disagreeable about some parental requests, but they do not argue about most rules.

II.   These children are at times bossy with their peers or siblings when they are playing together.

One child who had some strong-willed characteristics was Ginny, whom I introduced to you earlier. She was very assertive with her parents about wanting a later bedtime than her younger brother had, and the parents eventually made it a half hour later in order to avoid daily conflicts with her in the evenings. We saw in an earlier chapter that Ginny also had a learning disability that affected her at homework time. She was defiant about homework until her learning disability was addressed in school. The arguments with her parents centered on bedtime and homework, and once these issues were resolved, the conflicts with her parents were significantly reduced. Ginny did not argue with the parents about most other issues, such as coming to meals on time, putting away her toys, or getting dressed in the mornings. She did not disagree with her parents' rules about these things.

What about her treatment of other children? There were some signs of her being "bossy" with her brother and with peers; for example, she often "ordered" her brother to get ready faster in the mornings, and her best friend always allowed her to pick the game they played. Ginny liked being the leader with her brother and with her best friend.

With headstrong children, parents have a choice about whether to set a firm limit or compromise. If the issue is not critical to the parents, then giving some choice to the child will minimize conflict. It will also allow the child to feel proud that he made a decision for himself. In other words, pick your battles. What should you set limits for? Focus on what is important to you and to your child's social development. For example, highly aggressive behavior, like pushing or shouting when you insist on a bedtime, would be offensive to most people, but your child refusing to brush his teeth before school would be less offensive. You should focus more on the aggressive behavior. Eventually, when your child has learned to control his aggressive impulses, you can focus on less offensive behaviors. If you try to change too much at once, your child may feel overwhelmed, and you may not accomplish any of your goals.

One approach is to make a list of what your child does that is offensive to you, and then rank the items. What is most offensive to you is probably also most offensive to other people. This should be your focus. Now, the question is how do you set effective limits so that there are not continual conflicts?

Strategies for Headstrong Children

First of all target a specific behavior you want your child to change, like shouting at you, rather than something more general, like his negative attitude. It is more difficult for a child to stay focused on a general attitude than on a specific behavior. Also by picking a concrete behavior it will be easier for you and your child to assess whether he is making an effort to change. Next you should determine how often in a week's time your child expresses the negative behavior, in this case, shouting at you. You could use the behavior chart in chapter one, if you like, to record incidents of shouting. Then set a goal to reduce the frequency rather than to eliminate it entirely. If the shouting occurs about specific issues or at specific times of the day, like bedtime, you could insist on less shouting at this time, rather than try to monitor the whole day. (Notice that I suggested you set the goal as a reduction in shouting to start. After the child shows progress over a few weeks, then you can ask for a greater reduction and eventually an elimination of his shouting at you.)

Once you've set the goal, the next step is to motivate your child to try to attain it. The key is finding the right mix of incentives and negative consequences, which you will impose based on your child's progress. The incentives and consequences have to be things that your child cares about, or else your child will not be motivated to change his behavior. The incentive(s) and consequence(s) are best applied each day, so that the child sees immediate results. After the day is over, the child begins from scratch and tries to earn the incentive(s) again. This way the child will be motivated to try each day. By the way, do not talk a lot when you impose a consequence, because talking is a form of attention for your child, which may inadvertently motivate him to engage in the negative behavior again. Let the incentives and consequences, rather than your words, send your message!

The incentive should be something you will do with your child only if he earns it. This way the child will try hard to obtain it. If you like to engage in an activity with your child no matter how your child's day went, then do not pick this as the incentive. Also, it is a good idea to vary the incentive every few weeks, or have the child pick from one of several possibilities each day, so that he does not become bored with the incentive. It needs to be appealing in order for your child to keep it in mind during the day and try to earn it. Possible incentives include playing a card game with you, earning extra television or computer time, going to the park, riding bikes together, or extending bedtime a little bit. It depends what your child cares about, and sometimes it is trial and error to figure out what truly motivates a child, so do not feel bad if you do not hit upon an effective incentive right away. Remember that the number one reward for most children is their parents' attention.

Sometimes all you need to do is offer verbal praise right when your child has cooperated with you, and your child will be more likely to cooperate again

One mistake we all make with our children sometimes is to ignore good behavior and pay attention when our children are misbehaving. Who hasn't been busy with something around the house and failed to notice when their child was doing something we have wanted? It is easy to forget to praise a child when you are preoccupied with something else. The problem is that your child is less likely to cooperate in the future if you forget to praise him. If your goal, for example, is a reduction in shouting at meals, then it is important to comment on your child's talking in a normal tone of voice while you are at the dinner table. This will reinforce your child and make it less likely he will shout to get your attention. You could say: "You are speaking to me in a calm way. I really like that."

Behavior change can occur more quickly when parents use both incentives and consequences. Some parents have heard that consequences might harm a child's self-esteem, or make a child angry or depressed. Consequences do not harm children unless they are excessive or mean-spirited to the point of being abusive. The great majority of parents know what is abusive and what is not. Taking away television or video game time is not abusive. Neither is limiting phone time, nor grounding your child from going outside to play. Consequences are effective tools parents can use when setting limits. To stop using consequences would lessen the effectiveness of behavioral strategies.

A very useful consequence is to withdraw your time and attention immediately following a negative behavior. Remember that the thing children usually care about the most is their parents' attention. If you withdraw your interest and ignore your child for a few minutes, and then pay attention when his behavior improves, you are using a powerful technique to modify your child's behavior. For younger children especially, you might try ignoring your child and become temporarily "deaf" as a negative consequence, rather than take away some game or activity. This also can work with some teenagers who like to argue. What you choose as a consequence depends on what you think will work best to motivate your child to change.

The effectiveness of withdrawing your attention is the principle behind why "time-outs" are effective. During a time-out, the child sits somewhere by himself and receives no attention for a few minutes. This is similar to what happens if you ignore your child's behavior, except that for a time out, your child has a designated place to go to. If you decide to use this consequence, consider where would be the best place to send your child for a time-out. If the time-out is in his bedroom where there are plenty of toys, it may not be as effective as some boring place in your house, like the foyer, where there is not much to do.

When parents utilize a time-out as a negative consequence, it also has the benefit of providing the child a quiet time to calm down, which is useful if the child has been upset. What should you do if a child's behavior has not been defiant yet, but the child is beginning to get loud or emotional? Should you use a "time-out" so that your child has a place to settle down? In these situations, a child has not broken any rules yet, so you do not want to call for a time out.

Instead, you could establish a "chill" place somewhere in the house. You could explain that this is not a punishment, but just a time for your child to relax. If you decide to do this, do not also use the "chill" place when you are punishing your child. Use a different location for time-outs. For example, your child's bedroom could be for "chill" time, and the foyer, or stairs, could be for time-outs. In addition, it is important to present the idea of "chill" time when everyone is calm, not when you are angry with your child. You could ask your child to think about where in the house he might "chill" or "take five" the next time he feels frustrated and wants a break. See if you can agree on a place. Explain that you may also take "chill" time once in a while. If you decide someday that you need a break, and you label your decision to go to your room as "chill" time, you are modeling this behavior for your child. It is more likely your child will someday want to do so as well. However, your child may not think of it by himself for a while, so you could calmly suggest it when you see things are heating up. If your child refuses, you could walk away or just stop interacting with your child until he settles down.

A question parents often ask about behavioral strategies is how long to use incentives and consequences? Generally speaking, it is recommended that a behavior modification plan continue until the child has met the behavioral goal about eighty per cent of the time, for a two week period. When the child has reached this goal, the parent can increase the expectations if the original goal was only a partial reduction in the negative behavior. Once the final goal has been achieved, parents should gradually wean their children from the rewards: offer the incentive intermittently, once every few days, and then if your child continues to reach the behavioral goal, try to eliminate the incentive a few weeks later.

Sometimes the problem behavior recurs, and then a behavior modification plan needs to be re-imposed.

What if you are having no success? What if the behavior you have targeted is not decreasing in frequency at all? In this case, you could do one of two things: either you could change the incentives and consequences you are using if you think they are not meaningful enough to motivate your child, or you could adjust your goal and accept a partial change in your child's behavior if you think it might be too difficult for your child to change all at once. The first step usually is to change the rewards and consequences, because often what we think would be reinforcing is not something the child really cares to earn. If this does not work, the second step would be to accept a partial change in your child's behavior at first. In an earlier example we targeted shouting as the problem we wanted to change, and we could work on this goal in several stages. First we could ask for less frequent shouting (for example, if your child shouts several times a day, you could allow one mistake), and once this goal is reached for at least two weeks, then we could require an elimination of shouting. Or, rather than focus on the frequency of shouting, you might want to initially target the shouting of certain offensive words, like swearing, but allow shouting if more acceptable language is used. Once your child meets the initial goal, we could ask for no shouting at all.

One more suggestion for applying behavior modification techniques to the defiant behavior of a headstrong child: when trying to eliminate one behavior, suggest an alternative that is acceptable to you and that the child is likely to use. For example, if you want your child to stop shouting at you, allow him to say something like "I need five" or "I need to chill." Or if you think your child would prefer to express his anger directly to you, suggest an alternative he might use, such as "I don't like this" or "Come on." However, this only works if your child can leave it at that, and does not keep at you for the next fifteen minutes! Think about what will work for your child. Your goals are more likely to be met if your child has an alternative that fits his personality.

With older headstrong children, you can sometimes engage them in a discussion of what would be an acceptable alternative. Only do this if your child is relatively calm and not already shouting at you. A way to engage him without provoking a negative response would be to say something like: "We have a dilemma here. You want to do _____, and I want _____ because I worry about _____. How are we going to solve this?" The purpose of this intervention is to suggest to your child that you can have a legitimate difference of opinion, and that it is important to try to work together to solve differences. If your child participates in reaching a compromise, he is more likely to cooperate with you. If he cannot come up with a possible solution that you both can live with, you might suggest one or two alternatives. See if that engages your child in a discussion. If your child can work with you, instead of against you, you have made progress in reducing his defiance.

In addition to setting effective limits with your headstrong child, it is very important to admire some aspects of his personality as well. Admiration has a powerful effect on a child's self esteem because children so much want their parents to admire them. Since headstrong children tend to butt up against adults at times, it is important that there be some situations where parents admire their skills. Most headstrong children demonstrate persistence and determination; therefore, you should try to find a situation where your child's persistence is admirable and tell him that. For example, if your child is persistent in one of his activities, such as a sport, an artistic activity, or even a computer game, admire how his hard work pays off. This will encourage him to continue to work hard toward his goals. Positive feedback helps to build your child's self-esteem and balances the negative feedback he will receive at times for being headstrong.

Chart #5.2: Strategies for Parents

I. **Behavior modification strategies for parents:**

A. Pick one of your child's behaviors that cause conflict with you at home.

B. Observe how often that behavior happens each day for a week's time.

C. Set your initial goal as a reduction in the behavior rather than elimination of it.

D. Pick an incentive that your child can earn each day if he achieves the goal. Incentives should be some brief activity or small reward that your child is interested in, and something that you have the power to withhold; that is, the incentive only occurs if your child earns it.

E. Pick a consequence that your child will receive each day if he does not reach the goal. Consequences should be brief, but meaningful to your child.

II. **Other strategies for reducing arguments:**

A. Do not argue back. Become temporarily "deaf."

B. Have a nonverbal signal that it is time for your child to go to his "chill" place, or announce that you are going to "take five," and thereby separate yourself from your child.

C. If the situation has not yet gotten too heated, comment on what each of you wants and why, and then say: "I wonder how we can solve this." Try to engage your child in reaching a compromise.

Anger Overload

In 2001, I wrote an article for *Attention!* Magazine about a problem I called "anger overload." Children with this problem will erupt with rage and stay riled up for up to an hour at times. They have difficulty settling back down. The problem may happen when these children are asked to do something they do not want to do, such as a chore, or when they are prevented from doing an activity they like, such as playing their favorite video game. The problem may not happen for days at a time, but when it does, these children can say horrible things in anger or even become physically aggressive, such as hitting or throwing things at their parents. If parents try to explain anything at these times, the children usually escalate further. It is as if the rational parts of their brains are turned off temporarily. This problem does not meet the criteria however for a mood disorder, like bipolar disorder, nor any other diagnosis in the DSM-IV manual.

When anger overload occurs in children who are also headstrong, there can be intense outbursts when parents say no to something their children want to do. Not every headstrong child has this emotional reaction, in fact most do not. However, if your headstrong child does experience bouts of anger overload, his expression of defiance can become extremely emotional and sometimes violent. There can be screaming, crying, swearing, and/or physical displays of aggression. It is best to say as little as possible, and to leave your child alone at these times, unless he is hurting himself or someone else, in which case you may have to physically restrain him. If you ignore your child's outburst, within thirty minutes the level of anger usually eases, and your child will become more reasonable again.

I see this phenomenon usually in young or pre-adolescent children. One theory is that the emotional part of their brain, the limbic system, becomes overheated, and a related theory is that the rational part of their brain, the frontal cortex, has not developed enough yet to control their emotional reactions. To some extent, all of us can get like this occasionally. If our buttons are pushed enough, and especially if we are already stressed out by other problems, we can say some pretty awful things when we are angry. Once we calm down, we usually realize we overdid it and feel somewhat guilty for what we said when we were angry. The difference for children with anger overload is that it happens more frequently, sometimes more than once a week, and the expression of anger can be more aggressive than for most adults.

Parents wonder what to do if their child experiences anger overload. As I have mentioned, it is best to leave your child alone and not say much while he is in this state. He is not rational and will not respond to your comments in a rational way, but will probably escalate further. What parents should focus on is not what to do after their child rages, but how to prevent anger overload from occurring. The key is to anticipate it. Sometimes children overheat so quickly and unexpectedly that there is nothing you can do but wait it out, but sometimes you will observe patterns for your child. There will be certain situations when he is more likely to experience anger overload. Make a chart for the next week or two of situations when your child overheats. Does it happen more often when it is close to bedtime when he is tired, or rather when he is frustrated because he has to stop playing video games, or does it happen when he cannot have his favorite food? These are some of the times when children I have worked with have experienced anger overload. Try to determine some of the times when your child is more likely to get overheated.

If you see a pattern, try to plan ahead and tell your child what will be happening ahead of time. Enlist his cooperation, and maybe offer an incentive if he handles the situation in a more "grown up" way. Using words like "grown up" may help because most children want to be seen as acting more maturely.

Another possibility is to think of a way around the problem. For example, if you know it is hard for your child to stop playing video games on school nights (because there is not a lot of time after dinner to play a game) then make the rule that there will only be video games on weekends. Or if the problem is that your child is more likely to erupt in the evenings when he has to do a chore, ask him to do whatever chores are frustrating for him earlier in the day when he is better able to handle it.

If you cannot plan your way around his outbursts, and you notice your child starting to heat up, try to distract your child by engaging him in an activity or discussion of something else that is fun or interesting for him. For example, if your child is getting angry about not having time to go outside to play, try a favorite card game (It's better to take a few minutes for a card game than to allow the anger to escalate.) or talk about one of his favorite subjects. This strategy is only possible though if you can catch his anger early before it reaches the point of overload. Sometimes this is possible and sometimes it is not. Your child may overheat so quickly (in a matter of seconds) before you can change the subject. Do not blame yourself then, but remove yourself from the situation and stop talking until your child calms down.

Another suggestion is to have a heart to heart discussion with your child at another time when everyone is calm. It is important that you wait until later in the day when everyone is calm and rational. Talk about an example of his anger overload, and together try to generate alternative strategies that he can use himself some day if he is becoming upset. Here are some possible strategies that your child might be able to use: For younger children, an engrossing activity is usually more likely to help them change their mental state than a cognitive technique. For example, playing a game together with you, or playing with the family pet may distract him. Young children sometimes feel better if they hug a stuffed animal or wrap themselves in a favorite blanket. Doing an activity works better for children than imagining it. Most children, when they are angry, have a hard time imagining a fun activity or remembering a more peaceful day. For adolescent children, it might be helpful for them to turn on their favorite music. See if your child has any ideas that might help, or ask him which of your ideas he likes best. The more involved he is in the planning, the better the chance he will try to use the approach when necessary.

Now for the bad news: Most children will not think about these strategies on their own when the time comes. First of all, most children do not plan ahead of time to avoid an outburst. Secondly, once they get emotional, their rational brain is overloaded with emotion. For most children, therefore, it will be up to you, the parents, to plan ahead to try to avoid meltdowns, or to try to use distracting activities to help your child stay in control.

Still, having the discussion with your child while he is calm can be useful, because it alerts your child to the problem and gets him to begin to think about it. Eventually, when he is not terribly worked up, he may be able to use one of the strategies and begin to feel more control over his anger. Over time, he may be able to manage his anger more often. If you think of the goal as your child learning self control over the long term, rather than changing immediately, then you will not be disappointed if it takes months or even years. Explain to your child that the goal is for him to become the "boss" of his anger. It will take time, but someday he will be able to do it. Children want to be able to be their own boss, so that using words like "You can be the boss of your anger" is an appealing way to talk with children about developing better self control.

Chart #5.3: What To Do If Your Child Also Experiences Anger Overload:

I.   Keep a record for a week to see if there is a pattern for when your child overheats.

II.   Ignore your child while he is having an emotional outburst.

III. Try to plan ahead to avoid meltdowns.

IV.   Use distraction if you can catch it early.

V.   Later, when your child is calm, help him see the pattern and think about alternatives.

What To Do and What Not To Do for Headstrong Children

1. The mistake parents make the most with headstrong children is to talk too much while their child is being defiant. Parents often try too hard to talk sense into their child. In the process, the child is getting their attention, and his defiance is likely to continue. Remember that actions speak louder than words. In other words, let the rewards and consequences do their job! If your child likes the reward and dislikes the consequence, then the defiant behavior should decrease over the coming weeks.

2. When you stop talking or reasoning with your child when he is misbehaving, your child will probably become more defiant initially in an effort to provoke a verbal response from you. Your child is not used to your silence, and thinks if he tries a little harder, you will respond to him. Try not to say anything, unless your child is doing something dangerous. This can be hard because your child may carry on for quite a while at first. Over a few weeks, your child will likely cut back his defiant behavior more quickly, because he sees that it does not get a response from you.

3. If your child does something dangerous, like strike out at you or at himself, you will need to restrain him. This is more likely to happen if your child is not only headstrong but also experiences anger overload. Get help from another adult if your child is big and strong.

4. If your child is headstrong and also has anger overload, incentives and consequences will not usually be effective once your child becomes emotional. At that point, he will not be thinking clearly. For these children, in situations of extreme emotion, distraction is more effective than rewards.

5. If your personality tends to be shy or more passive, you may have trouble setting limits and then sticking to them. Ask a relative or friend for help. Try not to cave too often, because then your child learns that if he gets "obnoxious" enough, he will eventually get his way. Then it gets even harder the next time your child is defiant.

6. Sometimes parents try to set too many limits with headstrong children. Some parents are too "controlling." If you have heard others say this about you, think about what rules you can soften.

Think about what is really important for your child's well being, and focus on those issues. Your headstrong child needs to feel in control of some decisions.

7.   Spend one-on-one time with your child when all of you are calm. Pick an activity you all enjoy. Sometimes parents ignore their child when he is finally quiet, because they need a break and because they want to avoid the possibility of another argument. However, it is when your child is calm that you want him to see that you enjoy being around him. It is important to reward your child's calm and cooperative behavior by being interested in your child at some of these times.

Chapter 6

Behavior and Mood Disorders

Assessment question: *You have determined that your child is not just strong-willed because he is defiant about many different issues and his defiant behavior can go on for a long time, sometimes hours. It is likely your child has a behavior or mood disorder. Here are some questions to help you decide among possible disorders that a defiant child could have. 1) When defiant, does he lose self control and become very emotional, or is he more lawyerlike in his arguments? 2) Also think about your child's mood when he is not being defiant with you. Is he friendly, even helpful, with adults, or does he usually seem annoyed or distant from adults?*

> In order to make the correct decision about your child's possible psychological disorder, you need to get a sense of what his mood is like when he is defiant and when he is not. You will see in this chapter that there are a number of disorders which a defiant child could have, and it is often his mood that will help you decide which disorder your child exhibits. It is important to decide on the correct disorder, because your approach will vary depending on your evaluation. If you think your child has one of these disorders, you will likely need to consult a mental health professional to help you with your child.

What if your child is more than headstrong? What if you find yourself arguing with him many times a day over many different issues? Or what if your child is having repeated, lengthy tantrums whenever he does not get his way? The tantrums are more frequent (several times a day is possible) and of longer duration (they can last for hours sometimes) than you would find for a child who occasionally experiences anger overload. It is possible that he has a psychological disorder that is contributing to his defiant behavior. Usually, headstrong children will be defiant only when they feel strongly about an issue. Ginny was a good example of this. She was adamant about a later bedtime but did not argue about other aspects of the daily schedule, such as when to come to dinner or when to wake up in the morning. If you find yourself facing outbursts or arguments several times a day or more over many different issues, your child might be exhibiting signs of a psychological disorder. I will now help you decide if your child's behavior meets the criteria for a more serious psychological problem. I will discuss the four most common childhood disorders in which defiance is a feature, and show you how to distinguish among them.

The four disorders are attention deficit hyperactivity disorder, oppositional defiant disorder, conduct disorder, and pediatric bipolar disorder. In the accompanying chart, I list the major criteria of each disorder, based for the most part on the *Diagnostic and Statistical Manual of Mental Disorders-Fourth Edition* (otherwise known as DSM-IV). Let's review each of them and explain what parents can do.

Chart 6.1: Characteristics of Possible Behavior and Mood Disorders of Defiant Children

I.   Attention deficit hyperactivity disorder (ADHD)

There are three possible types of ADHD. The characteristics must be present for at least six months:

A. Primarily Inattentive type: Having difficulty sustaining attention, making careless mistakes, being forgetful, not finishing tasks, difficulty organizing materials

B. Primarily Hyperactive-Impulsive type: Excessive and extraneous moving or fidgeting, talking excessively, always "on the go"

C. Combined type: Characteristics of both 1 and 2

II.   Oppositional defiant disorder (ODD)

Four or more of the following are present for at least six months *and* as a result your child's academic or social functioning has declined:

A. Often loses temper

B. Often argues with adults

C. Often refuses to comply with adult requests or rules

D. Often deliberately annoys others

E. Often blames others for his own mistakes

F. Often touchy or easily annoyed

G. Often angry and resentful

H. Often vindictive

III. Conduct disorder (CD)

A persistent pattern of behavior such that the basic rights of others and major societal rules are broken. There must be three examples in the last year (from any of the below categories), with at least one example in the last six months:

A.   Aggression to people or animals, such as initiating physical fights, physical cruelty to animals, using weapons to harm others, or sexually abusing someone

B.   Destruction of other people's property

C.   Theft of significant value, breaking and entering, lying to obtain goods or favors

D.   Serious violations of curfew and school attendance rules, such as not coming home at night (beginning before age thirteen), or truancy from school (beginning before age thirteen), or running away from home for long periods (beginning at any age)

IV.   Pediatric bipolar disorder

All three of the following have been present for at least six months:

A.   Acting impulsively for one's own pleasure regardless of the wishes or requests of other people. What distinguishes the *pleasure seeking* behaviors of these children is

1.   the *disregard* for social norms and

2.   the *revved up or driven* quality of their behaviors.

B.   Angry outbursts toward others who block the child's pleasure seeking behavior. These outbursts often last longer than a few minutes.

C.   Rapid cycling of mood, such that there can be fluctuations daily between expressions of excitement, rage, relative calm, and sometimes depressed mood.

The criteria for all but pediatric bipolar disorder come directly from the *DSM-IV manual* (1994). The characteristics of bipolar disorder come from Dr. Gottlieb's book: *Why is my child's ADHD not better yet? Recognizing the undiagnosed secondary conditions that may be affecting your child's treatment* (2006).

Attention Deficit Hyperactivity Disorder

Attention deficit hyperactivity disorder is characterized by distractability, impulsivity and hyperactive behaviors. Some ADHD children have all three of these qualities; some have primarily distractability problems; and some exhibit primarily impulsive and hyperactive behaviors. The latter group of children has the sub-type of ADHD known as predominantly "hyperactive/impulsive" ADHD. The children with primarily distractability problems have the "inattentive" type of ADHD, and the children with all three qualities of ADHD have the "combined" type of the disorder.

Typically ADHD children who are primarily inattentive get distracted in school, forget where they put things, and have trouble with organization. This can be frustrating for parents, especially when children get failing notices because of missing assignments, or when children forget to do their chores around the house. Parents feel like these children are being defiant because they often continue to forget things, even when reminded daily by parents or teachers.

ADHD children who are hyperactive and impulsive sometimes blurt out their reactions or thoughts without thinking. They annoy others with their ill timed comments. In addition, they have trouble sitting quietly. Parents may notice that their children are constantly moving around at meals, while teachers may remark that these children do things like tap their hands or their feet, get up out of their seat a lot, and talk to others when they should be listening to the teacher. Because their behaviors disturb others, and because they have difficulty slowing down, these children are often seen as defiant.

Many ADHD children are not "purposely" defiant. They do not aim to forget things nor do they "try" to blurt things out. Furthermore, their behavior is different from strong-willed children who are determined to get their way and who argue with parents about certain issues. By contrast, ADHD children are not usually argumentative. For example, they do not usually feel a need to defend themselves when adults are upset with them about their behavior.

Some ADHD children become defiant at times when they are pushed by adults to attend to a task that does not interest them. When parents or teachers expect an ADHD child to do a lot of homework, for example, the child may resist. He may remember what his assignments are, but not do them. If the child refuses to do homework or refuses to cooperate with adults in other ways for a period of six months, and if the defiant behavior significantly affects the child's grades on his report card, then the child would be diagnosed with another disorder in addition to ADHD, namely oppositional defiant disorder.

It is only when ADHD children have another problem, such as oppositional defiant disorder, conduct disorder, or bipolar disorder, in addition to ADHD that outright defiance becomes a major issue. Studies show that about 50% of children with ADHD have one of these additional diagnoses. It is important therefore to consider if your child has one of these problems in addition to his ADHD. In the next section of this book I will explain how to determine if your child has one of these diagnoses. First, I will briefly discuss how to help your child if he has ADHD.

Helping Your ADHD Child

If your child just has ADHD, consider the use of stimulant medication in addition to implementing a behavior modification system targeting his organizational problems (if he is distractable) or his impulsive verbal remarks (if he is impulsive). Check with your pediatrician or a child psychiatrist about whether medicine is indicated and which one to use with your child. Most children receive time-released stimulant medication. The advantage of time released medication is that children can take one pill in the morning and have it last for eight to twelve hours. Your child's doctor will usually start with a small dose and then adjust it as needed, until your child is better able to concentrate in school.

Behavior modification without medication is *not* usually effective. ADHD is a mild neurological disorder, and the proper medication will help your child stay more focused. The medication however will not "teach" your child to organize his school folders and backpack! This is where behavior modification strategies can be helpful. Incentives and consequences will help your child remember to do tasks like to use his assignment book or keep his backpack organized. These objectives can be accomplished with behavior modification, especially if your child's medication has brought him to the point that he can focus more. If your child is not so distractible, it is more likely that your child will be able to attend to the goals you set in his behavior plan.

In addition to targeting organization, a behavior modification plan can help your child learn to control impulsive comments and thereby get along better with other people. Medication usually helps ADHD children become a little more reflective, but some impulsivity often remains. Behavior modification can further reduce impulsivity. Remember to set your goal as a reduction in impulsive remarks, rather than a total elimination of these behaviors. First, use the charting method, which was discussed in chapter one, to figure out how often your child is rude or blurts out annoying comments, and then set your goal as an improvement, rather than perfect behavior. It is difficult for many ADHD children to always be organized or to be socially attuned in every situation; still with medication and behavioral interventions, there will be significant improvement.

With ADHD children, as with most children, it is important to have activities where they experience success and contentment. Even with medication, school may be a struggle for some ADHD children. Help your child find an endeavor that is not a struggle, and one that he enjoys. For example, some children enjoy music or drawing, and others enjoy a sport or outdoor activity (like fishing or bike riding). Think about how you can support your child's interest and help it become a lifetime source of enjoyment.

If you have begun medication and behavior modification with your ADHD child and he is still argumentative with you, then it is likely your child has an additional disorder, such as oppositional defiant disorder. There are other possible disorders that can co-exist with ADHD, such as conduct disorder and bipolar disorder, but oppositional disorder is the most common. In the rest of this chapter, I will explain how to determine if your child has one of these disorders, and what you can do to help.

Oppositional Defiant Disorder and Conduct Disorder

The hallmark of oppositional defiant disorder (ODD) is frequent arguments with adults. In order to be diagnosed with ODD, the defiant behavior must be present for at least six months. In other words, the problem is not situational, because it has persisted over time. The DSM-IV manual says that at least four of the behaviors listed under ODD in the accompanying chart must be present to make this diagnosis. Actually, if your child exhibits any of these behaviors on a regular basis, it is likely that you will observe many of the other behaviors as well, since the behaviors all overlap. For example, "often angry," "deliberately annoys," "actively defies," "often argues," and "often loses temper" could all apply to the same outbursts. If these were the only criteria for ODD, then many young children and most teenagers would be diagnosed with ODD. Many teens are argumentative on a regular basis. Do they all have ODD? How do you know if your teen or younger child really has ODD?

The DSM-IV manual tries to answer that question by saying that the behaviors must be more frequent than is typical for children of a given age, and must be severe enough that there is "impairment in social, academic, or occupational functioning." The definition is still somewhat vague, and can be interpreted differently by clinicians or parents. What qualifies as "impaired" academic, social, and occupational functioning? Most children do not have jobs, so there would not be a disturbance in occupational functioning. The other two areas mentioned in the DSM-IV are academic and social functioning. It is more likely you will see a decline in school performance than a problem with social interaction. The reason is that oppositional children are more likely to argue with adult authority figures, like parents and teachers, than they are with peers.

Most clinicians would define an impairment in academic functioning as a significant drop in grades, not just one or two semester grades dropping one level (e.g. B to C), but *most* semester grades dropping one level, or one or two semester grades dropping *many* levels. Notice that we refer to "semester" grades. These are grades on your child's report card, not the grade on a test or homework assignment. If your child does poorly on some of his homework, but "rights the ship" before the end of the semester, then his academic performance has not really declined significantly over the long term.

Another way some clinicians define impairment in academic functioning is frequent misconduct that requires significant disciplinary action by your child's teacher, dean, and/or principal. Many children are disciplined in school at times, but oppositional defiant children challenge rules on a regular basis, such that they would receive detentions, and possibly suspensions, more often than their peers. Discipline does not slow their oppositional behavior very much, if at all. Furthermore, often the children who are disciplined frequently do not care much about their school work, so that their grades tend to be poor as well.

You can see that children who truly have ODD defy adults so much that it interferes with their success in school. These children become so intent on doing the opposite of what adults want that they "shoot themselves in the foot" academically. They would rather defy adults than be successful.

There is really a continuum rather than a hard and fast difference between headstrong children and oppositional defiant (ODD) children. Oppositional children argue more frequently with parents on a wider range of issues. In the beginning chapters of the book I asked you to chart your child's behavior, and I introduced you to Sam and Ginny.

Sam is an example of a child who has features of ODD, unlike Ginny who is considered headstrong. Whereas Ginny cooperated with adults on most matters, Sam would argue with and defy his mother on almost every issue. He would not come to meals, he would not answer her questions, he did not want to go out with her, and he did not respect her rules in the house. Over time, he began to argue with a couple of female teachers who he felt were strict and demanded a lot of him, similar to how he felt about his mother. This change occurred gradually, because Sam got along with all of his teachers through sixth grade. In seventh grade he complained about one of his teachers, and stopped doing a lot of the homework in her class. By eighth grade, he felt a couple of his teachers had "stupid" rules, and several of his grades slipped below C's due to incomplete work. Sam's behavior met criteria for ODD when his grades declined toward the end of junior high school. What began as a conflict with his mother escalated into a conflict with female teachers and a serious decline in his academic performance.

Further along the continuum of oppositionality is another disorder called conduct disorder. Conduct disorder (CD) is more extreme than ODD because major societal rules are broken, such as destruction of property, stealing (expensive items), leaving home and truancy. These children are defiant by disregarding the most basic expectations of parents, and usually of other people as well. Conduct disorder children may get into physical fights with peers, or physically harm pets. They do not argue as frequently as oppositional children, but they defy parents by their utter disregard for some rules that most children adhere to. To make this diagnosis, according to the DSM-IV manual, there must be three or more incidents of the behaviors listed in chart 6.1 over a twelve month period.

George, who was introduced in the beginning of the book, had some qualities of a conduct disorder, but did not quite meet the DSM-IV criteria. He did steal food from a convenience store, but to be considered a sign of a conduct disorder, the items must be of significant value. Also, though he was truant a few days in high school, to meet criteria truancy must begin before age thirteen. The truancy and stealing were violations of social norms, but not severe enough for him to be labeled CD according to DSM-IV's definition. The drinking and pot use did not meet criteria for CD either, but were signs that George had the beginnings of a substance abuse disorder. When confronted about his behavior George did not deny it, nor did he get into an argument with his parents. He remained defiant, but in an unemotional way. He just said he would do whatever he wanted regardless of the consequences. This kind of defiance is closer to a CD child than an ODD child, since ODD children are more argumentative. George is on the border between ODD and CD, closer to CD.

Many children with ODD or CD have additional problems, such as ADHD and learning problems, or their parents may have emotional or substance abuse disorders. It is important to figure out what the other problems are because if you address these accompanying disorders, your child's defiance will likely lessen. These secondary issues are like added fuel for your child's defiant behavior. If your child receives help for his ADHD or LD, and then experiences less humiliation at school, he is more likely to get along with his teachers, rather than defy them. Furthermore, if he succeeds in school there will likely be fewer conflicts with his parents about grades and homework. If in addition, the parents address any problems they are having with their marriage or with their own emotional health, there will be even less stress in the home environment. Less stress means less fuel for conflict and less risk of oppositional behavior.

I wondered whether George had any learning disabilities. He had said one of the reasons he sometimes skipped school was that he "hated" being there. Now that is not a good reason to miss school, but it made me wonder why he hated it so much. Was it because he did not like following the rules and felt bored in the classes? Or did he hate it because he had undiagnosed learning problems? George had never been tested, and I recommended we contact his teachers to find out if they felt he had difficulty learning. The teachers reported that in their opinion George did not try very hard, and as a result he was missing a lot of work. His grades were poor and had been so since junior high. I wondered whether he had been bright enough to get by in elementary school, but if he had mild learning disabilities he might not have been able to succeed in junior high when the work became more difficult. Unfortunately, the parents decided not to have him tested, so we won't know the answer.

Chart #6.2: Strategies for Working on Underlying Behavior and Mood Disorders:

I. **ADHD:**

  A. Consult with a child psychiatrist or pediatrician about medication.

  B. Work with the school to develop a behavior modification plan that addresses attention and organizational issues. Be realistic. Don't try to "fix" all the child's organizational problems.

  C. Encourage an extra-curricular activity that the child enjoys and where he experiences some success.

  D. Determine if the child has a secondary disorder, like ODD, CD, bipolar disorder or a learning disorder.

II. **ODD and CD:**

  A. Some adult needs to form an alliance with your child.

  B. Work on a behavior modification plan together with your spouse, and for severe problems, enlist the support of other adults in the community.

  C. If there is defiance in school as well, enlist the help of the staff there.

  D. Encourage relationships with those peers who have respect for society's main rules, even if these peers are not perfect "model" citizens.

  F. Determine if there is also a learning problem or ADHD.

III. **Pediatric bipolar disorder:**

  A. Consult with a child psychiatrist about medication.

  B. Ask the school for an IEP (individualized educational plan).

  C. When developing a behavior modification plan, focus on those behaviors that are more dangerous to your child's physical and emotional well being.

  D. Establish a "chill" place in your house.

  E. Teach your child how to recognize changes in his mood.

Strategies for ODD and CD Children

To reduce the defiance of ODD and CD children, parents will need to be firm at times and to reach out at other times. Limit setting without also building an alliance will lead to many angry confrontations with your child without a significant change in his behavior. Your child will likely rebel if he does not also have a rapport with you. On the other hand, developing a rapport without enforcing some rules will not be effective either. Your child will take advantage of you if you do not stick to any of your rules. ODD and CD children need some rules enforced, but they also need to feel cared for and respected. Let's now go into more detail about how to utilize both these approaches.

Helping Your ODD Child

I suggested some behavior modification techniques earlier to deal with headstrong children (see chapter five). These strategies will also be helpful if the child is in the early stages of ODD. Children who argue with adults but still attend their classes and obtain mostly passing grades will likely respond to limit-setting and incentives. Rather than repeat all the features of effective behavior plans which were presented in chapter five, let me highlight the key elements: it is important to use incentives and consequences that are short term and that your child really cares about. In addition, you could suggest that you and your child utilize "chill" time if either of you becomes aggravated with the other. Then, after everyone is calm, encourage your child to work on compromises with you. Ask your child to think about what would meet his needs and also take into account your concerns. If your child participates in the planning, he will more likely accept the compromise. Coming up with acceptable alternatives can help head off future struggles with your child.

When you have the first discussion about what your child wants to change, pick an issue about which you are willing to compromise. If there is an issue, such as curfew, which you strongly feel should stay the same, do not put it up for discussion, at least not until the time comes that you and your child have developed more trust in each other. Instead choose a topic, such as how much television your child watches or how much time he spends on the computer, which is probably not "life or death" to you. Your concern about the television may be that your child not neglect his studies or the family, but you probably do not care too strongly that the television viewing be restricted to an exact time limit. So that is open to negotiation. Let's say you decide to choose this topic to talk about with your child. Begin the discussion by asking him what he wants to watch on television. Once your child has spoken, in a calm way explain what your concerns are. Ask your child if he can think of a compromise. If he cannot come up with one, then you could suggest one. In essence, what you are doing is showing your child how to negotiate rather than get into an argument. You show your child that sometimes compromise is possible, and then you see if in the coming weeks, you each can stick to the compromise. You agree to look at how the plan is working in a week or two.

If your child would prefer to negotiate another issue which you do not want to put on the table, then do not be afraid to say: no, this is non-negotiable. Explain that there are some issues which you consider too important for your child's safety or welfare to negotiate at this time. Make clear that you are not trying to manipulate your child's life, but that you are concerned about your child's welfare. Non-negotiable issues could include making it to school on time; being home after school when there are doctor appointments; being home early on school nights. For each parent, the non-negotiable list may be somewhat different. It is really up to you.

You will need the help of other adults if your child's ODD is more severe, of if he has a conduct disorder. If your child is already failing his classes, leaving school without permission, and/or staying out all night without permission, then he may not accept your limits, but might walk out of the house instead of listening to you. If your child's behavior is defiant in so many ways that there is a severe academic or social impairment, parents usually need the help of their child's school, of mental health professionals, and of religious and community leaders to make a difference. Sometimes you might also ask the local juvenile police officer to help support the rules you set. Do not be embarrassed to ask for help of other adults with whom you or your child come in contact. The more all the adults work together, the greater the impact will be.

When a child is so oppositional that he comes before the juvenile court (for curfew violation, drinking in a public place, or for not attending school), parents may feel that they should help their child "get off." However, this would be counterproductive in the long run, because your child will continue to misbehave if there are not firm limits. The courts can be your ally in setting limits that your child will take seriously. Most children do not want to go to juvenile jail, and most judges do not want to send them there. But judges will insist on certain rules, such as going to school and being drug free, and oppositional teens are likely to take these rules more seriously if they come from a judge. Usually the court also assigns a juvenile probation officer to monitor the situation, and sometimes the child has to do a certain number of hours of community service. Parents should not be embarrassed that they cannot control their child at times. It is not your fault. There are biological factors, peer influences, and societal pressures that affect your child. It often takes "a community to help raise a child," and parents should take advantage of the help which the community provides.

Another group of adults who can be a critical source of support to you is the parents of your child's best friends. Your child spends a lot of time with his buddies, and if their parents are more lenient than you, your child will be more likely to argue with you about your rules. For example, if your child has a curfew of 11 p.m. on weekends, but your child's best friend has a curfew of 12:30, then your child is likely to think that your curfew is too early. Talk with the other child's parents and see if you share some of the same worries and see why they made their curfew later. If you can develop a rapport with the parents of your child's buddy, and if you can come up with similar rules (which may mean that you have to move your curfew closer to that of the other parents), you will have fewer conflicts with your child. Your son or daughter will be more satisfied if his rules are similar to his friend's.

Up to this point we have focused primarily on the establishment of rules with oppositional children. There is another critical step to helping these children learn to moderate their defiance. It is critical that some adult builds an alliance with your child. Sometimes that adult can be you, but sometimes your child is so angry with you that he is not ready to give you a chance. Think about whether there is some activity that you and your child both enjoy and that you could do together without an argument. You want to try to build a bridge with your child at a non-stressful time. Is there some recreational activity that you both enjoy, or is there a restaurant you both like? Would you both be willing to make time once a week to meet there?

If your child is continually rejecting of your efforts to join him in a non-controversial activity, then maybe there is another adult whom your child likes to talk with. Parents have to be the main "enforcers" and as a result your child may be angrier with you than with other adults. Your child may be more interested in spending time with a relative, like an uncle or aunt, or an adult from the community. Sometimes an ODD child will form a positive relationship with a coach, teacher, religious leader, family friend, or mental health professional. Do not feel badly if your child rejects talking with you at a restaurant but chooses to talk with his athletic coach after a practice. It is not because you are a bad parent, but because you have to set the rules at home which your child's coach does not have to do. Over time, the other adult, such as a coach, may be able to encourage your child to try harder to work things out with you at home.

The key point is that some grown-up reaches out to your child and that your child develops some trust in at least one adult. Your child will begin to see that adults can be allies, and will model the behavior of these adults over time. You may not see the results of your child's identification with adults right away, but it is a necessary step toward breaking the cycle of defiance with ODD children. Once your child forms a positive rapport with an adult, try not to say anything that might disrupt this relationship. You should not say too many nice things about this adult either. If your child senses that you want him to talk with someone, your child may do the opposite!

When speaking with an adult, your child is bound to find out that the adult sometimes has a different point of view than he does, but the adult does not lose respect for your child, nor vice versa. Your child learns that you can have a difference of opinion without getting angry. If they talk eventually about your child's school or social activities, he would likely begin to recognize that adults have concerns about his doing well in school, about showing respect to teachers, and about safety, and that his parents are not the only ones who worry about such things! Remember to let the relationship develop naturally. Do not try to get closer to the adult yourself at this time, as your son or daughter may perceive this as interference. This initial alliance with an adult shows your child that adults can be helpful even if they do not agree with everything he says or does, and your child's long entrenched attitude of defiance is thereby gradually reduced.

In the case of Sam, the ODD child we have been following, it was the therapist who was gradually able to form a rapport with him. The therapist empathized with his frustration with his mother's intrusiveness, and also took an interest in Sam's activities. Sam was reluctant at first to share much information about school and about his friends. He had developed a pattern of withholding information from his parents, which he transferred to the relationship with the therapist. Over time Sam found the therapist to be understanding, and he shared more.

The therapist also wondered out loud in a session why Sam's mother was so worried about him. The therapist asked Sam to consider whether his mother gets anxious about other family members as well. Sam and the therapist concluded that part of the problem was that his mother tended to worry about all of her children. In addition, the mother was especially concerned about Sam because of his declining grades in school. In this way, the therapist helped Sam to understand that there were reasons for the mother's behavior, other than her wanting to hassle him. The therapist suggested that in her own way his mother was actually displaying concern and love for Sam. The therapist tried to help Sam see that his mother's intentions were positive though her behavior was at times difficult for Sam to deal with.

In time, the therapist encouraged Sam to share a little information with his mother about his activities, and then to tell her politely when he wanted to stop talking. Furthermore, as Sam's trust in the therapist grew, the therapist was able to point out when Sam's remarks to his mother sounded provocative. He would become sarcastic or loud in the waiting room and in the therapist's office when the mother was present, and the therapist explained that this only aggravated his mother. The therapist made some headway, but unfortunately the parents withdrew Sam from therapy too soon. He needed the alliance with the therapist to last longer because he and his mother had not yet developed a consistently calm way of relating to each other. And there was no other adult whom Sam could talk with and trust. Without another adult to ally with, Sam's oppositional stance towards authority figures soon returned in full force.

Reach Out To Your Community To Help with Your CD Child

It is also important that a CD child develop a connection with some adult. However, it is usually even tougher for an adult to develop a rapport with a CD child, more difficult than with an ODD child like Sam. Conduct disordered children are typically so turned off to adults that they do not trust parents, teachers, or other professionals. CD children often feel like their parents and teachers want to manipulate them and that mental health professionals are in cahoots with their parents. Sometimes a non-professional, like the parent of one of your child's friends or some young adult neighbor, is seen as more trustworthy. The adult your child chooses may not be a friend of yours, and you may be wary of his influence on your child. However, the adult may turn out to be helpful.

There are two criteria that usually determine if another adult will be a good influence on your child. First, it is necessary that the adult has the time and interest, and second that the adult accepts society's values (like getting ahead in a legal manner). If such an adult has an interest in mentoring your child, do not be angry that your child listens to him and not you. Give it time. As I mentioned in the section about helping ODD children, do not try to get too close yourself to this adult early on, as your child may then become suspicious that you have co-opted his adult friend.

Once your child trusts one adult, he may eventually reach out to others, even you! Even if the adult "friend," or mentor, does not directly point out to your child that his hostility to you is excessive, your child's attitude toward you may eventually soften. Once your child sees that adults are not the enemy, your child may begin to realize that you really do care about him too. This process may take a year or longer, though, so do not expect quick changes. Sometimes your child's attitude toward you may not change until he is older and living on his own. At that point, you and he are no longer in conflict about the rules, and he may finally recognize that you care about him.

The most significant influence in your child's life is probably his friends. You might be able to have some effect on your child's behavior if you can get him to stay away from the worst peer influences. Try to determine who your child hangs out with and what these children are like. Do some of them show basic respect for you and for the law? If your child counts on you for rides, offer to drive him to the houses of peers who you think are more respectful of society's rules. Or, offer to take your child and one of his more respectful friends to a movie or the mall. If you know that some of the peers are active in gangs or get into a lot of fights in the community, or if they are disrespectful to you and other adults, do not allow them to come to your home. Your child will not like this, but has no choice but to abide by your decisions in your own home. Allow other more respectful children to come to the house, even if they do not conform to all of your standards. Your child will likely accede to your limits, because you are allowing some friends to visit. He would rather spend time with some of his friends than no one!

With George, the seventeen year old teenager who bordered on being CD, the issue of what to do about his friends was tricky. He never had them come over to the house, nor did he ask his parents to drive them anywhere. That eliminated the possibility of forbidding one of them from riding in the family car or from coming over to the house. The parents were not even sure if George and his friends hung out at his friends' houses or mostly on the street. The parents had been out of the loop for several years, and in hindsight wished that they had kept better tabs on George's activities beginning at an earlier age. The parents had allowed George from an early age to go out without saying where he would be. By the time teens reach sixteen or seventeen, it is late to start trying to influence their peer activities. From George's point of view, being with his buddies was very important; it would have been next to impossible to try to prevent George from hanging out with them.

George did not have an adult mentor, who might have influenced him to make better choices. He was not interested in being on any sports team, and the family did not belong to a religious or community organization where George might meet another adult who could take an interest in him. Not only did he want nothing to do with his mother and father, but he had no siblings.

The parents brought him to see me, and I developed a therapeutic relationship with George. I listened for several sessions to some of his problems with his parents, and empathized with his wish to be with his friends. I wondered out loud if he could be with his friends and not drink or take chances with the law. Could he have fun without drinking or getting high? We talked about his drinking and pot use; neither seemed to be increasing in frequency, nor were there signs of tolerance or withdrawal, which would have indicated the possibility of a substance dependence problem.

George had a court case coming up for underage drinking, and I reminded him that he should be extra careful to stay sober and to attend school regularly so that the judge would get a good report. I explained that the juvenile officer was likely to order a drug test before his court date, and probably do periodic drug screens for a year afterward if he was lucky enough to get probation. In addition, the judge would likely want to know if he was attending school regularly. I explained that this might make a difference to the judge when he decided on any consequences. I tried to point out what might benefit George without criticizing his behavior and without telling him to stay away from his friends.

In this case, the upcoming court date gave me and the parents leverage to influence George's behavior. He did not want to go to jail. The parents were smart to work with the juvenile officer, rather than try to protect George from the consequences of his actions. Hopefully, the judge would order a year of probation with periodic drug checks. This would help George stay sober. When tested for drugs after his arrest, there were no signs of cannabis. We were encouraged that George did not have a major drug problem yet. However, an extended period of testing would help balance the influence of his friends and would give George a reason to say no to drugs. We also thought that the judge might order George to attend an outpatient drug treatment program. This could help George learn more about the effects of drugs, and hopefully he would receive support from other peers in the program to stay sober.

With conduct disorder children, it is important to let the police and legal system do their job and help provide limits for your child. Conduct disorder children typically break the law at some point, either by fighting, stealing, selling drugs, or running away from home. If your child comes before the legal system, allow the courts to come up with a punishment that is fair and meaningful to your child. If that means court supervision, or community service, support the judgment. Significant jail time is another matter. Such a severe consequence may have more negative, than positive, effects. If jail time is involved, you must consider whether this is the only way to reach your child, as there are risks involved with having your child exposed to violent or dangerous youth while incarcerated.

Encouraging your teen to find a job is another way to influence his behavior. When I was meeting with George, I encouraged him to look for a job. George wanted to earn money towards purchasing a car. I explained to the parents that if George had a job, he might learn to be more responsible. I hoped he might respect his adult boss, and if his boss was decent to him, he might begin to see adults in a more positive light. In addition, in a job setting, he might meet new friends who did not drink and smoke pot. There is no guarantee that all this would happen, but I reached for whatever would get George engaged in the community in a positive way, and I hoped that a job might be a way to accomplish that goal. If indeed George did find a job, then he would also have less time to spend with his drinking buddies. On the negative side, he would also have more money for beer and pot, but I hoped he would save most of his money because he wanted to buy a car.

What if your child does not have a job, is not under court supervision, and there is no relative, neighbor, or boss whom he talks with on a regular basis? Another possibility is a residential school that works with CD children. Sometimes a residential placement is needed because it is the only way to break antisocial peer influences where you live. If some of your child's friends have similar conduct disorder issues, your child's defiance will only be reinforced by associating with these peers in your hometown. Initially, your child will fight going to a residential school, and won't trust the staff there, but over a period of months, your child will begin to depend on these adults emotionally and will begin to see some of them as fair-minded and worthy of respect.

Residential schools are very expensive. Another alternative is "job corps," which is a federal program to help older teens get a GED (high school equivalency certificate) and learn a career. The program is funded by the government and aims to get youth off the streets and into productive jobs. Your child would live on site with other youths in the program. Job corps will help if your child is ready to make something of himself. The program will not force your child to attend classes, and some teens drop out. However, it is a low cost alternative to helping your child turn his life around and separate from negative influences in the community. Sometimes what sells a child on trying job corps is being able to get away from you! However, leaving home will only work if your child also wants to change the direction of his life. Does he see that he is headed toward tough times without a high school degree and a good job? Is there someone in your family or community who can help him see that?

Bipolar Disorder

There is one childhood disorder which is similar to conduct disorder in some ways, but is actually very different and requires a different approach. This is pediatric bipolar disorder. These children are self-centered and pursue their own interests, like CD children do. However, CD children are motivated by material advantage or power, while bipolar children are motivated by immediate pleasure and often act quite impulsively. Bipolar children voraciously seek out pleasure, and appear "on the go" or "revved up" at these times. These children can become full of rage when their wishes are denied. Their defiance often takes the form of a tantrum or outburst, which often lasts less than an hour, but can go on for as long as several hours in some cases! Once the outburst subsides, these children can be cooperative, but when an important desire is blocked again, their rage will return. There can be rapid cycling during the course of a day, from calm to pleasure-seeking behavior, to rage, and back to calm. Sometimes during the relatively calm periods, there are signs of depressed mood (tiredness, irritability, or apathy). Periods of depressive mood do not occur with many bipolar children, though. What are more common are pleasure-seeking and impulsive behaviors alternating with angry outbursts. This spiraling of moods is unique to bipolar children.

The extreme mood changes are what distinguish bipolar disorder from oppositional defiant disorder and conduct disorder. I started this chapter with two questions to help you decide what your child's problem was: one question had to do with how your child acted when he was defiant: was he emotional or was he lawyerlike? The second question was whether he was friendly or distant from you when he was not being defiant. If your child is very emotional when he is defiant, but considerate of you when not defiant, the problem is likely bipolar disorder; but if your child is argumentative and has an annoyed or distant attitude with you most of the time, then he has ODD or CD. You will see later in this section that the approach for bipolar disorder is quite different than for ODD and CD.

First let me explain some differences of opinion that professionals have about the diagnosis of bipolar disorder in children. It is a fairly new diagnosis for children: it was not listed as a childhood disorder in the diagnostic manual DSM-IV, which was published in 1994. There is not yet a universally agreed upon definition for bipolar disorder in children, and this means different mental health professionals use somewhat different criteria to reach a diagnosis. One major difference is how extreme a child's pleasure seeking behaviors must be in order to use the bipolar diagnosis. Most mental health professionals agree that a bipolar child is drawn toward activities that are exciting and pleasurable, but some mental health professionals only use the diagnosis if the child is so set on his own pleasure that he takes dangerous risks in the process, such as when youngsters do bicycle tricks in the street without regard to automobile traffic, or when teens engage in sex with multiple partners in the same week, or drink to excess whenever alcohol is available. Other mental health professionals set the bar low, and make the diagnosis if there are repeated angry outbursts and some fluctuation in mood, even if the child is not driven to taking risks.

My criteria for bipolar disorder include some risk taking, but the risks do not have to be extreme and "dangerous." In order to be diagnosed with bipolar disorder, I also feel there must also be some angry outbursts (when the child's risky behaviors are blocked by adults). Behaviors are sometimes "risky" because the child is so intent on pleasure that he disregards danger at times. Another way of putting this is that the child wants something so badly that he does not consider the cost. This shows how preoccupied the child is with his own goals and needs. For me to diagnose bipolar disorder, then, the danger does not have to be extreme like when teens go on drinking binges, or when younger children do bicycle tricks in the streets while cars are whizzing by. Instead, a child may exhibit less dangerous, but still self-serving and hedonistic behaviors, such as running down the halls in school, playfully tapping other students in class, or "making out" with his girlfriend in between classes. The danger here is that the child will receive detentions and suspensions. Regardless of the level of danger, the key for me is that the bipolar child frequently acts impulsively to put his needs for excitement and attention ahead of the consequences.

In the DSM-IV manual, bipolar disorder is defined only for adults, not children. For adults, mental health professionals have considered the key criteria for the manic phase of the disorder to be grandiosity and elation. These are abstract words and fit better with the behavior of older adolescents and adults. I prefer other, more age-appropriate criteria for children. In order to reach a diagnosis of bipolar disorder in children, let me summarize how I would define mania: I look for repeated pleasure seeking behaviors that a) disregard social norms and that b) have a revved up, or driven, quality. This definition describes the behavior of children better than DSM-IV's terms: grandiosity and elation. My first criterion (a) substitutes for grandiosity, and I believe better captures the disregard young bipolar children have for other people's needs, while my second criterion(b) is a more concrete description than elation for how driven and "on the go" these children are.

For example, one seven year old child impulsively poked his classmates in an effort to stir up an interaction despite their lack of interest. The child continued egging on his peers by touching them until he got a reaction, when one classmate pushed him away. The teacher saw what happened and gave the impulsive seven year old a time out. The child proceeded to run around the room until restrained by the teacher's aide.

In this case, the teacher's aide had to take the child out of the classroom. The teacher's aide had to act because the teacher could not teach the other children while the bipolar child was bothering other students and running around the room. The child was brought to a "quiet" place in the social worker's office, but the staff did not talk with the child until after he had calmed down. If the staff had talked with him earlier, it would have "fed" the child's fury. While he was "revved up," the child likely would have argued with whatever they said. The problem is that these children can rage for a long time, and this is difficult for teachers or parents to manage. The key therefore is to try to prevent these rage outbursts from occurring in the first place.

Daniel, the pre-adolescent child whom I introduced in the beginning of the book, showed signs of bipolar disorder. Remember how Daniel kicked his mother's seat in the car when she would not take him to a fast food restaurant as he had expected. He proceeded to carry on for almost an hour. Here we see another key feature of bipolar disorder and that is the child's rage when his wishes are blocked. For many bipolar children, their expressions of rage can be dramatic and sometimes last for an hour or more. Their mood is so "revved up" that incentives and consequences will be of no help at this point. It is better to let these children wind down before talking with them. Parents should say little or nothing at all; just make sure your child is not harming himself or others. If your child does try to harm himself, you will probably need another adult to help you physically restrain him, and if there is no one to help, call 911.

In school, Daniel provoked a reaction from other students in whatever way he could because he thirsted for constant interaction with others. He told some of the boys that they were gay, and told some of the girls that they looked hot. When he was ignored by others, Daniel would escalate the interaction, often making additional rude remarks. Though the parents and teacher coached Daniel to refrain from making provocative comments, he persisted. Sometimes an aide needed to escort Daniel out of the room. He seemed to enjoy getting a reaction out of others, even if the reaction was negative.

For adolescents, there are risk-taking behaviors, including sex, gambling, or all night partying that is excessive for their age group. Bipolar adolescents are at great risk for unprotected sex and for excessive drinking because they do not consider the dangers to themselves or others. These adolescents, when in the manic phase, disregard their parents' rules as well as societal norms.

Helping Your Bipolar Child

First of all, for bipolar children, medication is very important to help them regulate their mood. By comparison, for ODD and CD children, medication is generally ineffective. The types of medication often recommended by child psychiatrists for bipolar children are mood stabilizers and/or atypical anti-psychotic medications. These medications help reduce the agitation and rapid cycling of bipolar children. Examples of mood stabilizers are Depakote, Lamictal, Lithium, and Tegretol. Examples of the atypical anti-psychotics are Abilify, Clozaril, Geodon, Risperdal, Seroquel, and Zyprexa. Most of these medications have been approved by the FDA for adults, but not for bipolar children yet. They are often used with children however because it is difficult to modify the behavior of children with bipolar disorder without medication.

Parents and doctors need to weigh the risks of side effects of the medication with the risks of not treating the child's emotional problems. How much are the problems harming the child's education, the child's relationships, and the child's self-esteem? Will psychological strategies alone help the child? For most bipolar children, there is little improvement without medication. When a child responds to the medication, he can better control his moods, and, as a result, he can then focus more on his work in school, and he can also interact more appropriately with other people in his life. Since these are relatively new medications for children, it is important that your child be monitored by a child psychiatrist, someone who is familiar with the dosage range and possible side effects for school age children.

Daniel did not improve despite a year of psychotherapy. Trials of ADHD and anti-depressant medication were ineffective as well. A new psychiatrist tried him on the atypical medication called Seroquel, and there was a marked improvement in his behavior. The doctor kept the dose low to avoid side effects like tiredness and weight gain. The frequency of physically aggressive outbursts was reduced to one in a six month period. In addition, Daniel was more cooperative about doing his homework. This was a significant change. Unfortunately the provocative comments in school were not greatly reduced. He still received time outs for talking in class, and we continued to coach him to avoid making annoying comments to peers. Our interventions were not successful until Daniel was put in a smaller class where there was greater adult supervision.

In addition to medication, bipolar children often require more supervision in school, and one alternative is smaller, special education classes. The medication usually helps, but does not work perfectly, and often there is still some moodiness and some impulsive, risk taking behaviors. In a class with two teachers and ten, or fewer, children, it is more likely that the staff can monitor the child's moods and act to prevent some of his outbursts.

In Daniel's case, when he was moved to a smaller, special education class, the teacher and aide could see when Daniel interacted in a provocative way with another student, and could give him a hand signal to stop and get back to work. Because the teachers were able to observe Daniel acting up as it happened, they could often intervene before he became overheated. If Daniel did not slow down, the aide could take

Daniel to a different room with a mat where he could lie on the floor and physically unwind. The aide was instructed not to interact with Daniel in this room, because a conversation could lead to an argument when Daniel was in a revved up state. Furthermore, we did not want this "chill space" to become a place where he got a lot of attention, because it might inadvertently reward Daniel's outburst. Once he calmed down, Daniel would return to class. The combination of medication and close supervision made a big difference in Daniel's behavior.

Some bipolar children can attend regular classes when they are in better self-control. However, many of these children will still need an aide to be present in the regular classes. They may over-react to some comment made by another child or they may become frustrated with their work, and an adult needs to be able to redirect these children quickly before they "overheat". For example, a child may find part of an assignment frustrating, such as a math problem, and rather than ask for help, he may act up. Or the child may laugh and make sarcastic comments when another child in the room makes a joke or makes a mistake. The aide can try to intervene before the bipolar student gets too loud or agitated. The aide may be able to distract the student or help him use a strategy to calm down. What Daniel's aide did was simply to put up her hand like a stop sign. Daniel knew that if he continued to disrupt the class, he would be taken out of the room. Without an aide, the teacher's options are more limited.

At home, minimizing changes in routine and minimizing other family members' emotional reactivity to the child's behaviors will help the bipolar child to stay in self-control. Most bipolar children have a difficult time coping with arguing and tension in the home. If you are in conflict with your spouse or with one of your children, it is important to try to work out these problems quickly, especially when your bipolar child is present. It is also important that other family members learn what bipolar disorder is and learn how to react calmly to the child's provocations. Family members do not have to give in, but should quietly ignore provocations rather than become enraged themselves. In addition, having predictable schedules for bedtime, meals, and showers will reduce surprises that sometimes can upset your child.

When their manic behavior is under control, these children can be warm and considerate. It is actually easier for adults to form a positive rapport with bipolar children than ODD and CD children. Bipolar children seek the attention of adults and are not so argumentative.

Their defiant behavior is more episodic. It occurs when they want something right away and cannot have it.

The behavior modification strategies we discussed earlier with headstrong children can be applied to bipolar children especially *after* medication has been used to lessen the child's level of emotional arousal. Behavior modification will usually not work well with bipolar children who are untreated medically because their level of emotionality will often be so high that they do not pay attention to incentives and consequences. Also keep in mind that whether children are medicated or not, behavior modification will not work when children are in a rage or in a revved up state. However, behavior modification techniques can be used before a child gets into a rage, and may help prevent an angry outburst from occurring. The goal of behavior modification would be to further reduce those pleasure-seeking behaviors that cause conflicts with other people or that are dangerous. Use the chart described in chapter one to determine which issues provoke the most defiance in your child. There will probably be several areas where your child's interests conflict regularly with yours. Think about which area of your child's behavior is the most risky to his physical or emotional well being. Focus on that area first, as you will not be able to reduce all risk-taking or self-centered behaviors at once.

For example, if your younger child takes risks by skate boarding in the streets, or your older child regularly violates curfew and experiments with alcohol, think about how to motivate your child to take better care of himself. Are there incentives that your child really cares about so that he would reduce his risky behavior? Possible incentives for teens would be gas money or use of the car. Sometimes, the challenge in motivating older children is finding an incentive or consequence that is short term and meaningful to them. If your child does not really care about the incentive or consequence you choose, it will not work to motivate his behavior. Then try to think of a different one.

Explain when your child is calm that you want him to have fun *and* be safe. Show him how serious you are by offering safer alternatives that still allow your child to do some of what he enjoys. For a child who likes skate boarding, offer to take them to a skate board park, and for a teen who likes to hang out with his friends and drink, offer your house as a place to hang out, but without the alcohol. Try talking with your teenager, and see if you both can come up with fun activities, such as a bonfire, a cool sound system for his music, or food his friends like.

These ideas are not always fun for the parents, but it is preferable to worrying about your teen going out and drinking!

Use consequences like grounding your child, if he chooses instead to violate your rules about safe behavior. If your older child does not respect being grounded and leaves the house without coming home by curfew, do not be afraid to call the police. Remember to use your community's resources to show your teenager that you are serious. Usually after you have called the police one time, your bipolar teenager will not walk out again when you ground him.

Bipolar children have a difficult time regulating their moods, even when they are not being defiant. There are several other psychological strategies that can help these children calm themselves down. It is often useful to establish a "chill" place in the house where everyone leaves them alone until they are calmer. Pick a day when you and your child are sitting around, and introduce the idea to your child. Explain the advantages of using this space. Mention that it can be any room in the house where he can retreat to if he feels himself revving up. There will be no consequences for taking time to "chill." Sometimes it is helpful to offer an incentive if your child uses the chill place to calm down. This may motivate him to try the idea. Initially, your child will probably not think to use this place, and you will need to suggest it when you notice your child getting agitated. However, if your child is already at a very high level of anger, it will not usually be possible to get his cooperation to do anything, including going to the chill place. At that point, try to withdraw yourself and allow him to chill wherever he is. The important thing is that your child settles himself down. Try again another day when your child is less agitated to encourage him to find a "chill" place before he gets overheated.

Daniel's parents suggested he use his bedroom as his "chill" place. They explained that they would use the words "chill time" when it was time for Daniel to chill. At first Daniel was reluctant to go up to his room when his parents gave the signal. The parents added an incentive of an extra half hour of video game time in the evening if he used his room to chill. Then Daniel began going up there most days on his own because he wanted to earn the video game incentive. Though the parents did not feel Daniel was always upset when he took chill time, they did not question him about that. They were pleased that he had begun using his room more to relax, and did not want to make a big deal about whether it was always needed or not. The parents decided to use the incentive for many months because Daniel continued to want to earn it. The parents did not mind because the incentive was something they were comfortable with Daniel doing in the evenings anyway, and it did not take extra effort on their part other than to monitor the amount of time. The parents set a timer in the kitchen, and when it went off Daniel was trained to stop the video game within three minutes, or he would lose some time the next day.

Parents usually need to cue children to take "chill time" because bipolar children are often unaware that their moods are changing. These children will start revving up, and everyone in the room is aware of it but the children themselves. Therefore one useful goal with these children is to help them become more self-aware. One way to do this is to establish with your child a verbal label for each level of emotional upset that he goes through. There are different ways to label your child's energy level; one is to use the colors of a fire. When your child is calm, you could say: you are at the blue level, and when your child begins to get excited you could say: you are at yellow. Higher energy stages are orange and red hot. Your purpose is to come up with a concrete label that will help your child begin to recognize his emotional state.

It may take months for your child to become knowledgeable enough about his own moods such that he could give you an accurate answer if you asked him what color he was at. So for several months, you gently label for him when his mood is "firing up." This strategy will pay off in the long run. Some day it will help your child identify changes in his mood, and in addition it may help him adjust his mood to a calmer state. For example, one day when your child is heating up, you might be able to say: you are at orange; let's see if you can bring it down to yellow. Your child may try to do so because he wants your approval; however, remember that once his arousal level is too high it may not be possible for him to change it without other assistance, such as from his medication or by spending time "chilling".

It usually takes a few months for a child to become comfortable with whatever labels parents use to describe his mood. Make sure you have used the labels for a while before you ask him to try to change his emotional state. When you finally ask him to try to change the "color" of his mood, pick a time when he is not too agitated so that there is a greater chance of success. Once he gets better at regulating his mood, you could try asking him to do so when he is at a higher level of emotional upset. Do not be punitive if your child is unable to do so.

Another strategy that eventually builds self-awareness is for you to use the chart from chapter one to write down the sequence of behaviors that leads to an angry outburst. Chart several outbursts. Is there a pattern? Is there an issue that often leads to your child's rage, such as being told by you that he cannot have friends over to the house because it is late, or hearing from friends that they are busy and cannot play with him? If you see a pattern you can talk with your child about it when he is calm. Then when the issue comes up again in the future, like when your child is going to ask a friend to come over, you can warn him that the friend may be busy, and at the same time offer to play a game with him if his friend cannot play. In this way, you are trying to head off your child's rage by anticipating possible disappointment and presenting an alternative that he would enjoy.

With bipolar children, it is important for parents to be flexible and realistic. The strategies I have outlined do not usually work immediately. If you are persistent and if you have limited goals at first, you and your child will begin to reduce conflict. When your child is calm and you want to introduce a new strategy, put it in a positive context: explain that you care about him and his safety. You could say that you want him to have fun, but still be around to take care of *you* when you are old and gray! Levity helps to defuse tension and improve cooperation. (Actually in this case it may be true that you hope he will be able to take care of you someday!)

For many bipolar, CD, and ODD children, you should consult with mental health professionals who can help you come up with a good behavior plan and help you improve your relationship with your child. Because children with these disorders are so challenging, it is recommended that you seek out the advice of a professional in your location who has experience with these childhood disorders. This professional may be able to develop a positive rapport with your child and/or suggest ways that you and your child's teachers can do this. The professional can also help you determine if there are secondary conditions, like ADHD, LD, or other family issues, which may be affecting your child. Many children with CD, ODD, or bipolar disorder have secondary conditions, and if you also work on these problems, you will have a much better chance of reducing your child's defiance.

Depression Does Not Cause Defiance

Bipolar disorder is very different from depression. In bipolar disorder there is more extreme fluctuation in mood, from manic excitement, to rage, to relative calm. Bipolar children become extremely aggressive when their wishes are blocked by adults. By contrast, depressed children are usually not aggressive. To the contrary, there is usually apathy and a loss of energy to participate in normal everyday activities. Many depressed children feel worthless and hopeless about the future. Some depressed children are irritable at times; however, the irritability generally takes the form of occasional whining and complaining, rather than the uncooperativeness and argumentativeness which is characteristic of defiant children.

If depressed children act defiantly, it is because they also have another problem which brings on the defiant behavior. For example, some depressed children have an underlying personality structure that is strong-willed. Others have a disorder, such as oppositional defiant disorder, while still others are going through situational changes, such as separating from parents during the teenage years. Their defiance is due to these additional problems rather than due to their depression. When I encounter depressed children who do not have additional situational or structural characteristics associated with defiance, then they are passive and apathetic, and not argumentative. There is no defiance at all.

What To Do and What Not To Do

For ODD and CD children:

1. You are going to have to lower your expectations somewhat. That way you won't stress out every time your child breaks one of your rules. Your child will act out and not listen to you. If you expect him to follow the rules most of the time, you are probably going to be disappointed.

2. Think about when you and your child disagree. What do you feel the most strongly about and what can you let go of for the time being?

3. When your child is oppositional, think about what is a proportional response on your part. Vary your response, so that your child realizes that some behaviors are more serious than others.

4. Do not be too generous with your money, especially if you do not like what your child is spending money on. Also, if your teen wants money, he may do things around the house to earn it (You now have some leverage!) or he may go out and get a job. A job can be a great learning experience. If your child gets

a job and wants to keep it, he will need to learn to control his anger and accept the authority of his boss.

5.   If there is a school activity like a sport your child is interested in, encourage this even if it takes away time from his homework or from helping you at home. A sport or other school activity is another opportunity for your child to learn respect for adults, in this case, the coach. For ODD and CD children, remember that it is crucial that they learn to develop respect for some adult.

6.   It is hard to find something to do together with oppositional teens, but it is critical that your child form a bond with you or some other adult. Is there some activity that you and your child can do together once in a while? (Everyone has to eat! Is there is a restaurant you both like?)

7.   With some ODD and CD children, they will not respect your rules unless the police and courts get involved and back you up. Don't be embarrassed to let your local law enforcement personnel help.

For bipolar children:

1.   Teaching self-control is key for these children. You should model this behavior by staying calm yourself even when your child loses control.

2.   Try any method that helps your child take a break and chill when he is beginning to get angry. You can use humor, distraction, hand signals, silly gestures, or any brief signal that will help interrupt your child's mood. The signal will work better if it gets your child to smile, or think about something else. It is hard for a person to stay angry if he is laughing or if his focus changes from the source of his anger to something else.

3.   When everyone is calm, try explaining to your child how he could suffer if he does not control his temper. One way is to explain that his temper will "scare" away his friends. You can say that you want to help him learn self-control before other people see how he acts when he gets mad. If your child is concerned enough about what other people will think of him,

it may motivate him to try to control himself better. This is one way to show him the cost of his behavior.

4.   Medication is usually necessary for these children. If your doctor tries one medication and your child has side effects, talk this over with your doctor. You want to work with your doctor, and give him feedback about how your child responds to the medication, both positively and negatively. Based on how your child responds, the doctor will decide whether to alter the dose or change the type of medication. Unfortunately there is no way to know in advance exactly what your child's response will be to different medications. Be prepared to try several before hitting upon the right combination.

5.   Hang in there during your child's outbursts. Bipolar children's moods can be extreme and can last for an hour or more sometimes. Unless you catch it early and can distract your child, which is impossible to do on a regular basis, your goal is to ride out the outburst without anyone being hurt and without your child benefiting in any way from his behavior. Say as little as possible and try to do something else until your child calms down. You do not want your child to get your attention until he calms down.

Chapter 7

Problems in the Marriage or with a Parent

Assessment questions:

1) Is there continual conflict or tension between you and your spouse? The tension may be overt, in which case there will be frequent arguments, or it may be covert, in which case you might feel disinterested or lack empathy for your spouse. One way to determine if there are marital problems is to consider with whom you look forward to talking or sharing time with the most. Is it your spouse?

2) Does one parent have an emotional or substance abuse problem?

This chapter will be divided in two sections: one on marital problems, and one on emotional problems of parents. Either of these issues can lead to defiant behavior by your child. It is hard sometimes to be objective about your own behavior, but try to determine if you have a problem that could be affecting your child.

If you are having serious marital arguments or if you do not wish to spend time with your spouse, this could be a factor in your child's defiance. Your child may be angry with both of you for not "getting your act together." Children do not like it when their parents are in conflict. It makes the home less calm and comfortable. In addition, your expression of anger towards your spouse serves as a model for your child. In a sense, your message to him is that if you want to get your point across, get loud or disagreeable!

One way to assess whether marital problems might be having an effect on your child is to look over the chart (from chapter one) indicating what is going on at the time of your child's defiant behavior. Is there an argument between you and your spouse immediately before your child's defiant behavior, or possibly during the hour leading up to your child's defiance? Let's review the cases of Sam and Ginny, whom I introduced in earlier chapters. Sam became physically defiant with his mother about an hour after a dispute between his parents. On the other hand, we found no such correlation for Ginny. Her parents did differ at times, but not so loudly and not so often. Furthermore, when it came to discipline with the children, Ginny's parents usually worked together. Ginny knew she could not get one parent to side with her against the other, whereas Sam knew his father would likely side with him against his mother. This split between Sam's parents emboldened him to challenge his mother even more.

Problems with the Marital Bond

In the case of Sam's family, we see a more serious problem than occasional conflict between the parents. They despised each other, and even after they had divorced, they continued their conflict about the children. Not all marriages that end in divorce are toxic for their children. Many divorced couples work together when it comes to child rearing issues, and get along reasonably well once they are not living together. When divorced parents cooperate, there is less stress for the children and there is less likelihood that one or more of the children will become defiant.

Staying together in a difficult marriage is not a panacea for the children. There are many couples who do *not* divorce but have a hard time getting along, and this causes problems for their children. There is a greater chance of defiant behavior by one or more of the children if the parents never learn how to get along.

The marital problems may not always be exhibited in overt conflict between the parents, but by a cold stalemate. Parents may avoid interacting with each other as much as possible, and may hardly talk with each other even when the family is occasionally together for an activity or a meal. When the parents do speak with each other, there may be subtle ways that they undermine each other. For example, when the family goes on an outing, one parent may make a sarcastic remark about the other's choice of music on the car radio. Such comments by themselves are not toxic, but if sarcastic remarks are what characterize the little interaction that the parents have, then the tension will often be apparent to the children. Or in a restaurant, when one parent is disciplining a child for making too much noise, the other parent may smile, or wink, at the child. The parent's smile, or wink, could be interpreted by the child as support for him over the other parent. The timing of one parent's smile may undermine the effectiveness of the other parent's discipline.

One tell tale sign that your marital issues have affected your child's behavior is if your child is much more defiant with one of you than the other. In Sam's case, he would give his mother a hard time, but not his father. What had happened was that Sam had sided with his father against his mother. The father was the "good guy" and the mother the "bad guy." The father pretty much let Sam do what he wanted. The father did not ask a lot of questions when Sam went out to see his friends, did not regularly monitor Sam's homework, and did not insist on many rules in the home. When the mother tried to enforce a rule, Sam felt empowered to defy her. He knew that his dad would not be angry with him for giving his mother a hard time.

Occasionally despite a healthy marriage, one parent becomes the target of a child's defiance. This can occur when one parent does most of the child care, while the other parent is busy with work or other activities. Because one parent is often away from home, the child may think this parent would not agree with the other parent's rules. If the child does not have the sense that the parents are backing each other up, he may feel emboldened to challenge a parent's authority.

No matter what the reason for your child defying one of you more than the other, there is a simple and important rule to lessen your child's defiant behavior: work together. When you back each other up in front of your child, he will be less likely in the future to start an argument with one of you. If one parent is the target, the other parent should let the child know that his defiance is unacceptable to both of you. Reinforce this message when both of you are home. If you have any questions about why your spouse took a certain action while you were away, check with the other parent when the child is not around. In front of the child, you want to be a united front. This sends a clear message to your child that defiance will not be tolerated by either of you.

Sam's parents could not do this because of their strong dislike for each other. When the judge in the divorce proceedings recommended family therapy, the parents worked with the therapist for several months and learned to back each other up on several basic rules. They agreed on meaningful consequences when the rules were violated. There was a dramatic decline in Sam's defiance during this time. However, in the end, the parents were more interested in continuing their duel in court than in maintaining Sam's more respectful behavior. Their arguments gradually increased between sessions and even during sessions. The children were excused from the sessions at these times, but they could hear the parents arguing from the waiting room. The message was clear to the children:

we are so angry and distrustful of each other that we can't work together even when your welfare is at stake. I have observed this unfortunate state of affairs in several families over the years. Sometimes warring parents will call a truce if their child has a crisis, like a medical emergency or repeated truancy. But even then the truce may only last as long as the crisis!

The problems in Sam's family are an example of what family therapists call a boundary disorder. There is not a clear boundary between the parents and the child: the parents expressed more warmth toward their children than they did to each other, and when it came to disciplining the children, one parent sided with the children instead of with the other parent. In healthy families, the marital bond is primary, and the parents not only stick together for disciplining the children but also the intimacy between the parents is greater than the intimacy between parent and child. If a parent's primary source of support is not another adult, but one of the children, then there is a boundary problem.

When there is a boundary disorder, the parent and child alliance takes precedence, and the child often takes on the parent's feelings towards the spouse. Sometimes, this child literally speaks for the parent. For example, when one parent is angry that his spouse has been out all evening with her friends, the child may express the parent's anger by becoming defiant with the absent spouse when she returns home. The child may question the parent about her whereabouts or ask why she was gone so long. The timing of the child's outburst gives you a clue that the marital problems have contributed to the child's defiance.

In healthy divorces and in healthy marriages, the parents' bond remains strong when it comes to childrearing issues. There is mutual respect, and the parents trust each other when dealing with the children. If a child does not like the way one parent disciplined him, the child will not be able to talk the other parent into questioning how the first parent handled the situation.

The way to control your child's defiance is not only to work together when setting rules for your child. If you are having an ongoing conflict about the rules, it is usually a sign of a more basic lack of regard or trust you have for each other. You need to identify the source of your mistrust and work on building mutual respect. What is the reason you doubt the other parent? What are you really angry about? If you do not resolve the underlying mistrust you have for each other, then even if you resolve one disagreement about the children soon enough there will be something else about your children's behavior that serves as a focus for your conflict. Therapy for the adults is required to resolve the underlying feud.

If parents do not resolve their problems, not only will the child's defiance continue at home, but the child will eventually feel emboldened to challenge other adult authority figures, like teachers. The child may feel that the parent with whom he is allied will support him with teachers, especially if the teachers are similar in some way to the "bad guy" parent. Sam, for example, did not respect some of his female teachers, whom he felt were controlling like his mother. Initially the father was sympathetic with Sam, but when he realized that Sam's behavior and grades worsened as a result, he took a firmer stance with Sam about respecting his teachers. In order to be effective, Sam's father needed to give Sam this message repeatedly, because Sam felt his father would eventually see how "obnoxious" his teachers were.

Marital therapy is hard work. Parents often need to re-discover what brought them together in the first place, and work to build back trust and intimacy. It is easy to feel slighted by your spouse and pull away. It is much harder to talk through the hurt and try to take into account each other's sensitivities. Also, it takes a major time commitment outside of therapy to build and maintain a healthy marriage. There is no short cut to spending quality time together. Remember that your children will ultimately benefit if you take time to build intimacy with your spouse, even if that means taking some time away from your children.

Chart #7.1: Determining If the Parents Have a Problem

I.   Signs of marital problems

If there are marital problems, there will usually be two or more of these signs of trouble:

A.   Frequent unresolved conflicts with your spouse

B.   Lack of conversation with your spouse

C.   You enjoy doing activities more with your child than your spouse.

D.   Your child argues primarily with one parent only.

E.   When you discipline your child, your spouse often sides with your child.

II.   Signs that a parent has emotional problems

If there is an emotional problem, one or more of these signs will usually be present:

A.   One parent has conflicts with co-workers as well as his spouse and children.

B.   One parent prefers drinking to interacting with his spouse or children.

C.   One parent is continually advising the child and spouse about how to do things.

D.   One parent is distant from the family but occasionally becomes very angry without warning about an act of disobedience by the child.

Does One Parent Have an Emotional Problem?

Sometimes the marriage is basically sound, even if there are occasional differences which parents have with each other. However, one parent may have a personality type that clashes with one of the children. One example is a parent who is over-controlling. This parent wants to know everything about what a child is doing in school and with friends. The parent asks a lot of questions each day, and makes many rules about what the child should be doing during his free time. A related problem is with parents who are obsessive compulsive. These parents often have excessive requirements about punctuality or neatness. When parents are too intrusive about order and cleanliness, there is a greater chance that their children will feel angry and rebel.

Another kind of problem occurs when parents are alcoholics, workaholics, or depressed. These parents are usually distant and uninvolved in their children's daily lives, but may suddenly become over-involved when their children say or do something that catches their attention. They may then try to regulate their children's behavior, which causes conflict because the children are used to being on their own.

Some parents may not have a disorder, but may get moody when they have been chewed out at work or had an argument with a colleague. When in a bad mood, the parent may get on a child's case. For example, one parent came home one day and yelled at his child to clean up his room without warning. The parent threatened to throw out the child's toys if the room was not cleaned immediately. The parent may have talked about the mess in the child's bedroom before, but did not become angry about the problem until the day he was chewed out by his boss. The child became enraged, said he hated his father, and proceeded to slam his bedroom door shut.

In all these cases, we see that there can be a conflict with your child if your expectations are too high or if they are unpredictable. If the parent is obsessive, over-controlling, or alcoholic, then it is unlikely he will remain calm and set consistent limits. He may continue to criticize his child if the child does not comply perfectly with his demands. A conflict is even more likely if your child is strong-willed. Strong-willed children are more likely to resist. The resulting "collision" of wills can be deafening!

If a parent's personality or emotional state is part of the problem, not only will he have occasional conflicts with his children, but it is also likely that the parent will have problems with other adults. An over-controlling or alcoholic adult is likely to get on the nerves of his co-workers or friends at times. If you are unsure if you have a problem, ask yourself if you have alienated co-workers or friends, or if you have had trouble getting along with other family members.

Often, but not always, when a parent has a problem, it spills over into the marriage and causes marital problems. For example, if a parent needs the child to always be on time, then he probably expects this of his spouse as well. If his spouse does not feel punctuality is that important, then there is likely to be a clash. Or if the parent comes home in a rage from work, he is likely to take it out on the spouse, not just on the child. The spouse may be shy or may have learned to avoid his partner when he is in a rage, but the child may not be able to contain himself.

Think about whether you have been moody or hostile lately toward your spouse and children. Maybe your child's defiance is related. The problem with your child can be a wake up call to think about yourself. You might take this opportunity to meet with a therapist and explore how to improve your relationship not only with your child but with others as well.

Felicia's mother decided to seek psychotherapy because she was feeling anxious about her daughter's increasing closeness with a boyfriend. As her daughter spent more time with her boyfriend, she became more distant emotionally from her mother. The mother was having trouble sleeping at night and suffered some anxiety symptoms during the day, including periods of rapid breathing and heart palpitations. The mother recognized that her worries were getting out of control. The therapist helped her realize that she was missing the close relationship she had had with her daughter, and encouraged the mother to talk more with her husband and other adult friends.

The therapist also shared with the mother how worries about adolescent children are fairly universal, and that the key is to find a balance between setting limits and allowing children to make more choices themselves. The therapist helped the mother think through the pros and cons of different possible limits. The therapist also helped the mother realize that her daughter was pretty responsible, so that the mother could relax some of the rules. The mother no longer tried to limit the number of days that her daughter could see her boyfriend, but kept an evening curfew. The daughter appreciated the mother's trust in allowing her to see more of her boyfriend. Felicia wished she had a later curfew, but did not argue much with the mother about it. She was relieved that she did not have to try to lie about where she was going any longer.

Chart #7.2: What To Do If Parents Have a Problem

I.   **If there is a marital problem**

    A.   Try to separate parenting issues from your marital problems, and work together when it comes to the children. Try to come up with a plan for the children that both of you can agree with.

    B.   Work on your plan in private with the other parent. Try not to disagree about what to do in front of your children.

    C.   Do not discuss your marital disagreements with your children!

    D.   Avoid a rigid split in your roles where one parent is always the "good guy" and the other parent is always the "bad guy." Ideally, both parents will be able to set limits with their children as well as praise them. If one parent is always punishing the children, that parent should try to wait and let the other parent handle the discipline sometimes.

    E.   Get professional help when you are unable to follow these basic rules.

II.   **If one parent has a problem**

    A.   If your problem is interfering in your relationships with other people, try to figure out how you can limit the impact of the problem on your family. Can you see the problem coming, and can you delay it or get some time alone to settle down? If you have been getting angry or moody lately, you may be able to regain control if you can hold off expressing your frustrations while you are emotional.

    B.   If you cannot figure out the source of your problem or if you are having trouble changing your behavior, you should seek help. There are a number of possible resources you could choose from. You could speak with your family doctor, your religious leader, a therapist, or a support group of your peers.

While Felicia's mother was at times too controlling, she could adapt and became more flexible when she realized she was being too restrictive. She understood where her fears were coming from and was determined to manage them in a way that did not harm her daughter's growth.

In the case of Sam's family, the mother was unable to change. She was strong-willed and demanding with her son as well as with other people in her life. In Sam's case, she wanted to know who Sam talked with at school each day, what they talked about, what homework he had, and what grades he received each day in school. She would inundate Sam with these questions on the days she saw him after school. In addition, she was insistent that Sam keep to a schedule after school. Sam refused to follow the schedule, and also bristled when his mother asked him questions about school. Sam was provocative and oppositional with his mother. Within a few minutes, he and his mother would often be in conflict with each other.

Remember that there were other issues in Sam's family besides the mother's personality; there were ongoing struggles between the parents and there was Sam's oppositionality with other female authority figures, besides the mother. What was the cause of Sam's defiance toward his mother? Was it the mother's intrusiveness, Sam's oppositional personality, or was it the conflict between the parents? In real life, there can be multiple causes, and we may not know exactly how much each contributes to the problems with the child. No matter which came first, you usually have to work on each of the causes in order to reduce a child's defiance.

It is not unusual to see multiple factors underlying a child's defiance. Interestingly, Sam's oppositionality was not diagnosed until the seventh grade, which is also the time that the parents' conflict increased. Would Sam still have become oppositional if the parents had resolved their differences? We can speculate that the severity of the parents' arguments increased the chances that Sam developed oppositional defiant disorder. It is important to treat marital conflict before problems with your child develop. You can sometimes head off more serious problems for your child if you attend to your issues early on.

In the next chapter I will discuss in more detail what you can do when there are multiple causes of defiance. I will make recommendations about which problem to work on first.

What To Do and What Not To Do

If there are problems in the marriage:

1. Your children are innocent bystanders in your conflict with your spouse. If you put down your spouse, your children will be affected. They may get sad, or anxious, or angry. One possibility is that they will become defiant with you and/or your spouse.

2. Try to separate your spouse's value to your children from your feelings about your spouse as a marriage partner. Each of you as parents has something to offer.

3. If you are frequently feeling angry with your spouse about the marriage or about the children, then you should get some advice from a friend or counselor about how to handle your anger.

4. Do you think your child is better off if he sees less of your spouse? This is usually a sign of your hostility toward your spouse, and does not mean you should limit your child's activities with your spouse, unless your spouse truly has a serious emotional or drinking problem.

5. If you think your spouse has a serious problem, ask yourself if other more neutral parties feel the same way. Be careful that you do not jump to the conclusion that your spouse is sick and is damaging your children, because it may be that your belief that this is happening is the real problem.

6. Children want to love both parents. Who wants to grow up hating one or both of his/her parents?

7. Do not talk negatively about your spouse to your children and do not give any covert signs of disapproval in front of the children either. For example, do not wink, or smile, at your child while your spouse is disciplining him. Furthermore, do not go up to your child later and say that what he did to get punished is not really that bad. If you do these things, you will be undermining your spouse's authority, and this will likely increase your child's defiant behavior.

8.   If there is an ongoing struggle between you and your spouse, your child may feel pressured to side with one of you. The child may side with the parent who is around more, or may choose the parent who gives him more freedom. Or a child will side with the needier parent, because a child does not want to see either parent suffer. No matter who your child sides with, if your child is siding with one of you on a consistent basis, this is a sign that the parents' conflict has negatively impacted the child. Remember children do not want to take sides, but sometimes are subtly forced to do so by the level of the parents' dislike for each other. Children will take a side if they have to in order to get their emotional needs met.

9.   Don't blame your spouse if your child is defiant. It's always easy to blame someone else. Consider also what you may have done to contribute to the problem.

10.   If you are alone with your kids and one of your children breaks an important rule, try to consult with your spouse before you make a final decision about what to do. Your spouse will be more likely to consult with you if you do the same.

If one parent has an emotional problem:

1.   Parents often have inertia about getting help for themselves. They often feel that they do not have a serious problem, or that their problem is not affecting their kids. Are you being honest with yourself? Have you heard from other adults that you should get some help? Don't put it off any longer.

2.   If you have a substance abuse problem or have too much stress in your life, a mental health professional can help you get back on track. Even if you only lose control once in a while, that "once in a while" can be devastating for your children. Get some help for yourself, and you will be indirectly helping your children at the same time!

3.   If your spouse has a drinking or substance abuse problem and continues to deny that he has a problem, you might want to attend a support group, like Al-Anon. Check online or with a local mental health agency for Al-Anon meetings in your area.

People in these groups are going through similar situations, and will help you.

4. There may be similar support groups for teens in your community. Some high schools also offer support groups.

5. If you find yourself blowing up at your children over a problem that in hindsight you realize was not so big, ask yourself why. What was going on that day for you? Also ask yourself if what your children did to arouse your anger was similar to something you did when you were younger. Your blow-up could be due to old unresolved conflicts you have had or could be due to recent stresses during the last few days, or both.

6. If you figure out the cause for your blow-up, make a mental or written note about it. You may want to look over your notes when you feel stressed out in the future. If you know that what is bothering you is not really your children's behavior, you will be less likely to take out your frustrations on your children. If you make the connection before you blow up at your children, you have made a gigantic step toward controlling your anger. You may still have some anger about whatever your children have done, but you can separate out the part that has to do with other issues in your life.

7. If you figure out the cause of your over-reaction after you have already blown up at your children, apologize to your children when you have calmed down. Tell them that you over-reacted and that you are sorry.

8. If you feel yourself getting extremely angry with your children but do not yet know exactly why, try to delay your response for even thirty seconds. You will likely have better control of your behavior if you can get through the initial surge of emotion without saying anything.

9. If you have problems, do not give up on parenting your children. Withdrawing from your family when you feel a surge of emotion, or when you have been drinking, may be helpful in the short term, but in the long term it is better if you get some help. Your children need you around as a parent!

Chapter 8

What To Do If There Are Multiple Causes

> You have followed through with all the diagnostic questions in the book and you have determined that there is more than one cause for your child's defiant behavior. Furthermore, the book recommends a different approach for each of the causes. What do you do now?

For many defiant children there are multiple causes, and each one usually needs to be addressed if your child's behavior is going to improve. If each cause independently contributes to a child's defiance then each should be dealt with at about the same time. However, there are occasions when one cause exacerbates another. If the "aggravating" condition is resolved, then the other issue may be less of a problem. In these cases, the primary "aggravating" cause should be worked on first. Let's look at some scenarios where there are multiple underlying causes and see how you might handle them.

A Situational Cause Combined with the Child's Personality

First of all, there can be a situational stressor combined with a structural one. For example, a child can experience a loss of your attention due to a change in your work schedule and at the same time the child may have an underlying personality that is headstrong. If the structural problem is a headstrong personality, and not a severe disorder, like oppositional defiant disorder, then usually it is wise to address the situational stressor first. By addressing your child's concerns about the change in your work hours, you may be able to lower his frustration; if he is less frustrated his headstrong personality will likely not come into play as often. Stress exacerbates personality traits. A headstrong child, for example, will become even more single minded and less flexible when under stress.

However, if the personality issues are severe enough to be considered a disorder, such as oppositional defiant disorder (ODD), then you will need to come up with a strategy that takes into account the ODD as well as the immediate situational stressor. Addressing the situational cause will not reduce the ODD behaviors to a significant degree. ODD is a personality disorder that usually has been present for a year or more, while a situational stressor, by definition, has only been present for a short time. The child's oppositional defiant disorder brought about significant conflict with adults before the more recent situational factors began, and there would likely continue to be conflict even if the situational stressor were resolved. An example would be a young teenager who has a history of oppositional behavior, and in addition he joins a new peer group that has a late curfew. The situational stressor is the "pressure" from his peers to stay out as late as they do. Your teen wants to have the same privileges as his friends. He now argues incessantly with you for a change in his curfew. There is the situational cause of peer pressure added to the teenager's usual defiant personality. Since the teen's defiance is partly due to ODD, it will not stop even if you resolve the curfew issue.

In this case, the parents will need to re-double their efforts to form an alliance with their teen. Developing an alliance with ODD youth as well as developing a meaningful behavior modification strategy are keys to resolving conflict with them. Review the section of chapter six that discusses how to resolve problems with ODD youth.

It is also important to think of a way to resolve the situational stressor, which in this case is peer pressure to have a later curfew. Think about the purpose of your curfew, and whether you can alter the time and still accomplish your purpose. For example, you may be worried that your child will stay up late and drink, and that you will be asleep and unable to check on him if the curfew is much later. Can you think of an alternative that will balance his wish to be with his friends and your wish that he not drink? One possibility would be to make the curfew a little later, but also insist that your child wake you up when he comes home if you have fallen asleep. This way your child would know that you will be checking on him no matter what time his curfew is. Discuss the possible solution with your spouse first, and once the two of you agree on a plan, then discuss it with your child.

If your child does not want to compromise with you, it is possible that another adult, whom the child sees as more neutral, such as a school counselor or family therapist, may be able to help. Your child may listen more to a therapist about the importance of compromising. The therapist would try to explain to your child that he is getting a lot of what he wants, and that he does not have to give up a lot in return. It is not easy to work out conflicts with ODD teenagers. It can be a very difficult and explosive time when an ODD child reaches the developmental phase of adolescence and becomes more influenced by his peers. Don't be embarrassed about reaching out to community resources to help you and your child.

A Situational Cause Combined with the Parent's Personality

Sometimes, one of the problems may not be the child's personality issues, but the parent's. There can be a situational cause, such as a teenager wanting more alone time to spend with friends, that interacts with an emotional problem of one of the parents. For example, some parents have trouble allowing their teens to separate and make more decisions on their own. These parents can be very loving and often have done a great job raising their child when the child was younger. But during adolescence conflicts may arise in part because the parent wants to hold on tight to their teen and not allow him as much freedom as the teen wants. This can make the period of adolescence particularly stormy for the parent and teen, because the teen wants more independence while the parent cares more about keeping the teen close to the family. For instance, the parent may insist on the same curfew the teen has had for years, and may also want the teen home to have dinner with the family most nights, even on weekends. However, the teen may resist because he wants to spend some nights out with friends.

This issue occurred with Felicia and her mother. Felicia wanted to spend more time alone with her boyfriend away from home, and the mother wanted her to stay in the house most nights. The mother was afraid her daughter would have sex with her boyfriend if they were alone a lot, and the mother also longed for the days when she would spend evenings talking with her daughter. The mother would not extend Felicia's curfew because she felt Felicia would be more likely to be alone with her boyfriend then. In addition, the mother did not want her going to her boyfriend's house because the boyfriend's parents allowed them to be alone in the bedroom with the door closed. Felicia grew increasingly defiant as the mother held on tight to her daughter.

In this case, it was helpful to meet with the mother first and understand what her concerns were before the mother and daughter tried to resolve their differences. The mother learned that she was holding on too tight in part because she missed the closeness she had shared over the years with her daughter. The mother was used to talking with her daughter in detail about her life and spending many evenings with her at home, while her husband worked late. The mother was encouraged to share more of her feelings with her husband and with her friends, and to expect less time with her daughter. The mother was able to separate her needs from the needs of her daughter. Once the mother made this shift, she was able to think through what kind of limits made sense for her daughter. She allowed her daughter to spend more time with her boyfriend, and extended the daughter's curfew somewhat. She also discussed with her daughter her concerns about the daughter's sexual involvement with her boyfriend.

When a parent's problem is not severe and can be resolved in a short time, it is wise to start there. If on the other hand the parent has a major emotional or substance abuse problem that has been going on for years, it is unlikely to be resolved quickly. In that case, the parent should start to get some help as soon as possible, but in addition someone should meet with the teen and help him to think through how to deal with his parent. Ask the teen if there are there ways to get some of what he wants without coming into open conflict with his parent. For example, if he wants to stay out late, can he arrange in advance to sleep over at a friend's house, so the friend's parents will be responsible for monitoring the situation, rather than the emotionally disturbed parent? Or if the parent has a substance abuse problem, the teen can be taught to recognize when the parent is under the influence and can be encouraged to avoid "heavy" issues when the parent is not sober.

It also may be helpful for the family to meet altogether with a therapist, and for the therapist to serve as a mediator for discussions in the family. Sometimes, parents, even those with alcohol abuse or other problems, will be able to listen better to their teen if a third party is present. The therapist might be able to show family members how to figure out each other's underlying concerns and teach them not to rehash the same arguments over and over again. However, it is also possible that the troubled parent may be inflexible or remain too critical of the teen until the parent gets some help for his problem on his own.

One Cause Is the Child's Personality and the Other Is the Marriage

If the child has a more longstanding problem, such as oppositional defiant disorder, and in addition there are significant marital problems, then you and your spouse should first try to resolve your own issues of mistrust and anger. One suggestion would be to work with a marriage counselor to find the source of your marital problems, and then try to develop a strategy for your ODD child that you both can agree on. If you can improve your marital relationship with short term marital therapy (of about ten to twenty sessions), it is worth doing this first and then approaching your child's issues as a united front. If you do not work on your marriage, it may be hard to come up with a behavior plan for your child that you both can agree on. Furthermore, even if you were to agree on a plan, you may not trust your spouse to implement it when you are not there. For a behavior plan to be effective, it is important that the spouse who is not home supports the actions taken by the parent who is dealing with the child. An oppositional child may very well attempt to get around one parent's rules by appealing to the other parent who is not home. You need to work with your spouse so that your child cannot divide and conquer! It is hard to do this if there is ongoing marital strife.

Sometimes the marital conflict is longstanding and hard to resolve. After trying for several months, you find that you and your spouse still do not agree on how to discipline your child. In that case, it becomes necessary to begin other interventions for your ODD child, such as individual counseling. Therapy for your child may help him understand how his anger increases when you and your spouse have a dispute. Another reason for starting the individual counseling sessions is that it takes time for a therapist to develop an alliance with an oppositional child, and this means it will take time for therapy to be helpful.

In Sam's case, I started out working with the parents to try to develop a unified behavior plan. It was difficult because each parent had different ideas about what Sam's problems were, and furthermore they did not have trust in each other's parenting skills. The mother felt that the father had no rules and that he encouraged the son to disregard what she had to say. The father felt his ex-wife tried to control everything in Sam's life and that he was more reasonable in his approach to Sam. Within a few weeks, it became apparent it would take months for the parents to learn to trust each other's parenting abilities. The level of anger and mistrust between the parents was extreme.

In the meantime we decided that Sam needed to see a counselor individually. He needed to form an alliance with an adult whom he might trust, and building rapport was going to take some time. He had little of substance to say to the therapist early on in therapy, because Sam did not trust that the therapist would care about his point of view. After all, he had learned from the parents' conflicts with each other, that adults were more focused on their own battles than on him.

Over several months, we made progress with Sam and with the parents, and the conflicts between Sam and his mother decreased. A year later, however, the alliance between the parents broke down when the mother challenged the custody arrangement in court. At this time, the parents stopped communicating with each other, and Sam's defiance toward the mother surged again. Sam stopped going over to the mother's house, and neither parent moved to resume the visits. In addition, Sam's performance in school worsened: he went from one F to three F's on his report card. Despite the increase in Sam's defiance at home and school, the parents refused to work together while they were battling in court about custody. The parents stopped meeting together with a therapist, and the parents also stopped taking Sam for individual therapy.

As you can see, in complex cases, you have to work on all the causes of defiance, but sometimes there are limits to what therapy can do when there are ongoing legal disputes. It would have been ideal if the court had intervened in Sam's case and required the parents to continue to work together with the therapist. When the parents had been motivated to work together on Sam's defiance, there was a decrease in Sam's acting out behaviors. Sam's behavior regressed once the parents' cooperation totally broke down.

Two Structural Problems within the Child

There are some cases where there are multiple structural causes existing in the child, but none in the family. If each cause independently contributes to the child's defiant behavior, then each must be addressed. If you remove one problem, the other will still be there. However, as you make progress with one problem, it sometimes makes it easier to make headway with the other. This is because there is a tendency for problems to interact, such that the stress from one problem aggravates the other. For example, Ginny had learning disabilities and a headstrong personality, and both of these contributed to her defiant behavior. The school evaluated her learning problems and offered individual and small group academic help. At the same time, the parents brought Ginny to a therapist who met with her and also advised the parents about how to deal better with Ginny's headstrong nature. Once Ginny began receiving help for her learning disabilities, it lessened the frustration from school work. Because she felt less stress about school, she was in a better mood after school, and it made it a little easier to work on the conflicts at home which arose from her headstrong personality, such as the conflict about her bedtime. Interestingly, once a compromise was reached on her bedtime, the teachers reported that Ginny's mood and concentration improved in school, and she became more cooperative with her learning disabilities teacher! The progress at home had a positive effect in school and vice versa.

What if a child with learning disabilities also has a behavior disorder like oppositional defiant disorder (ODD), instead of a headstrong personality? It will still be important to work on both the learning disability and the ODD symptoms in order for the child's defiance to lessen. The main difference with an ODD child compared to a headstrong child is that improvement in ODD symptoms is more gradual. Also, the ODD child is likely to be more resistant about getting help for his LD problems, because ODD children are more argumentative and more resistant to what adults want them to do. ODD children may not cooperate with an LD teacher.

Not only do ODD symptoms make it harder to work on learning problems, but the learning problems can aggravate a child's oppositional disorder because there will be more stress between the child and his parents if the child is struggling in school. The parents will be frustrated about the child's poor academic performance, and thus more likely to snap when their child is argumentative, and at the same time their child will be more moody and argumentative if he has had a hard day at school!

Once a child receives help for learning disabilities, parents may be better able to make inroads with the child's defiant behavior. In other words, you still have to address the child's defiance but it may be easier once the learning problems have improved. LD (and ADHD also for that matter) fuel the child's feeling of failure and thereby fuel his defiance. Take away some of the fuel, and you will have a smaller fire!

When One of the Problems is Bipolar Disorder

If there are two structural causes within the child, and one is a mood problem like bipolar disorder, then it is important to address the mood disorder first. Some children have bipolar disorder and a personality issue, like oppositional defiant disorder. Bipolar disorder makes oppositional issues worse. Bipolar children are so revved up and impulsive that their conflicts with adults tend to be longer and louder. It is important to get the mood disorder under control first then. Pediatric bipolar disorder usually requires medication. You will not be able to make many behavioral changes in school or at home until the biological issues of the mood disorder are addressed. Once the child's mood is more stable, you will better be able to make inroads with the behavioral components of the child's defiance.

In summary, we have seen that the relationship between multiple causes of defiance can be complex. When there are multiple causes of defiance within the child, you must decide if one cause is "aggravating," or exacerbating, the other. If so, address the "aggravating" condition first. Or, if one cause can be more quickly resolved, start with that problem. If both causes are long term and contribute independently to the defiant behavior, then both causes need to be treated at about the same time.

Chart #8.1: What To Do First If There Are Multiple Causes

I.   **A situational cause combined with long term issues related to the child's personality**

   A.   If the structural problem is that your child has a headstrong personality, then deal with the situational cause first.

   B.   If the structural problem is a more severe psychological disorder, work on it and the situational cause at the same time.

II.   **A situational problem combined with a parent's emotional problems**

   A.   If the parent's problem is not severe, help the parent first.

   B.   If the parent's problem is long term, then meet with the child at the same time that the parent gets help for himself.

III.   **Problems with the child's personality and the parents' marriage**

   A.   If the marital problems can be improved in a short time, start there.

   B.   If the marital problems are severe and may not be resolved soon, then begin work with the child at the same time that the parents try to resolve their problems.

IV.   **Two structural problems within the child**

   A.   If one problem is with learning or attention, and the other is a behavior disorder, like ODD, work on both at the same time.

   B.   If one problem is a mood disorder, and it aggravates a behavior disorder, like ODD, then treat the mood disorder first.

Chapter 9

The Diagnosis May Not Be What It Seems!

Sometimes you try one approach and after a few months there is no change in your child's behavior. You make some adjustments and still nothing. You wonder why. There could be another, less common, cause for your child's defiance. For example, sometimes there are past events in your family's life which might still be affecting your child many years later. Or sometimes one cause is so glaring that another possible cause is overlooked at first. In this chapter, we'll look at some possible "hidden" causes and advise you what to do.

When evaluating a new client, a mental health professional gathers information by asking himself many of the same diagnostic questions which this book has outlined. The professional thinks over whether there is an immediate situational cause or a more long term problem with the child or with the family. If the cause seems to be structural, rather than situational, then the professional evaluates whether the problem is due to the child's personality or due to issues with the parents. I have shown you which questions you should ask yourself in order to reach a decision about the cause of your child's defiance, and then explained what approaches work for each possible cause.

The information gathering phase does not really end when a diagnosis is made, however. As a therapist gets to know the child and family better, new information can emerge that can alter the diagnosis. Any diagnosis is provisional and hinges on whether the information which was collected is accurate and complete. We make the best decision we can, based on the information we have at the time. If new information comes to light that changes the child's diagnosis, then the strategies we use change as well.

Do Marital Problems Really Matter?

One factor which can affect the information we gather is how open and straightforward the parents and child are. Sometimes a child or parent does not trust the mental health professional with certain private details of their lives. Without an honest account of a family's life, we may come up with the wrong diagnosis. For example, the parents may not want to discuss their marital issues with the child's doctor, because they are embarrassed or because they fear the problems will escalate if they start talking about them.

Another reason why some information does not come up at the outset is because parents do not feel it is relevant to the child's current problem. The parents may realize for example that they had marital problems, but they may feel these problems are in the past. The problems may have been mostly resolved, and the parents might feel that their old marital issues have nothing to do with their current problems with their child.

Parents cannot possibly tell a mental health professional everything that has gone on in a family's life in a few sessions. Likewise, professionals cannot possibly ask every conceivable question in the first few interviews with a new family. There is always a selection process going on such that parents and the professional discuss what they feel is important and relevant to the current problem the child is having. Past events in a family's life may not seem relevant to the parents or to the professional at first and may not come up in the initial interviews. There are other more current pressing issues which seem to explain a child's defiance. And in fact many times the past events are not critical to the current problem. Events, such as a divorce or a major illness or death of a family member, are important in a family's life; however, the key question for our purposes is whether these past events are related to the child's current defiant behavior.

One important question to ask yourself is about the timing of the event in relation to your child's defiance. *Did your child's defiance begin around the time some past family issue or event occurred?* If so, then it might be relevant and needs to come up for discussion. For example, if the parents had considered divorce several years ago and if the child's current problems began around the time of the past marital tension, then the marital history needs to be considered as a possible cause. A child sometimes acts up when parents are in conflict with each other. The child may get worried about the parents staying together and may exhibit his worry by being irritable and defiant. The parents may have been preoccupied with their own issues at the time and may not have considered the child's behavior to be significant. As the months or years go by, other issues may have added to the child's defiance, so that now the original cause may be overlooked. However, the origins of the child's current behavior may lie in the earlier family discord. The child may still be worried about his parents' marriage even though the parents have resolved many of their problems.

To help determine if your child is still worried that the disagreements between you and your spouse will escalate into physical fights or divorce, ask your child the following questions. Pick a time when everyone is calm, and start with the first question in the following list. Proceed with the next question if you get a positive answer to the prior one:

1) Are you still worried about how Mom and Dad are getting along?

2) Do you worry we will get divorced?

3) Is there something you heard recently that worried you? Or do you still think about a time in the past when Mom and Dad had a big argument?

Hear your child out, and be understanding about how scary the past conflict was. Then try to point out what you did to improve your relationship with your spouse, and point out an example of how you are getting along better now (if this is true). If you are still having problems with your spouse, think about getting marital therapy. Ask your child to tell you when he gets worried again, and give him a hug!

If you recognize that there have been issues in your family's past or in your child's development that you initially overlooked, review the relevant chapters in the book. Try to determine whether this additional issue could be another cause for your child's defiance, and then adjust your strategy accordingly. For example, if you think marital issues could be affecting your child, re-read chapter seven, and consider what else you could do to reduce your child's defiance. Therapists make changes over time, and so should you!

Physical or Sexual Abuse

Another topic that parents and children sometimes overlook is if some years ago the child was abused physically or sexually. The parents or the child may be embarrassed about what happened, or they may feel that their child has already gotten over the abuse and that it is not necessary to get back into it now. Another possibility is that the parents or child cannot recall what happened in the past. People sometimes forget in order to protect themselves from the stress of dealing with a painful event. It is extremely stressful to face the memory of a trauma, such as sexual abuse.

It is possible that an earlier trauma has had a profound effect on the child or the family and has brought about a change in the child's mood or personality. Children who have been abused may experience various painful emotions, including fear, hopelessness, guilt, shame, and rage. In some cases, children may become more defiant toward adults. They may argue with adult authority figures, like teachers, or become passive-aggressive and ignore them. If the defiant behavior has been going on for years, then these children may be diagnosed with oppositional defiant disorder. See chapter six for a full discussion of the behaviors of oppositional defiant children.

It is also possible that abused children may completely reject society's values, and may develop elements of a conduct disorder. For more about conduct disorders, also see chapter six. In these children's minds, attending school and planning for their future becomes unimportant. They would rather stay out all night and get high with their peers, and in addition they might steal from their family, or from stores, in order to pay for their drugs. Immediate pleasure has taken precedence over any long-term goal.

It is not known exactly what causes some abused children to be oppositional or to develop a conduct disorder, while others experience more anxiety and depression. It is likely that the way a child copes with abuse depends in part on his underlying personality and in part on his other life experiences. Children who have been strong-willed from the early days of their childhood are more likely to become aggressive under a stress like abuse or neglect. If, in addition, these children have a peer group where aggressiveness is prized, then this trait is likely to predominate.

These scenarios are different than the usual way ODD and conduct disorder come about. Usually there are genetic personality components as well as moderate stressors in a child's life that bring on these disorders. The stressors are not usually as powerful as abuse.

With abused children, there is a different pathway by which oppositional defiant disorder can develop. There is a traumatic experience (the abuse) that brings about a change in a child's personality;

the child may not have been defiant at all before that trauma occurred. In a sense, the cause of the child's defiance is situational, but the situation happened months or years ago.

If your child was abused and has become oppositional, you would still use many of the suggestions that were outlined in chapter six for dealing with ODD children. However, you will also need to help your child deal with his feelings about the abuse. First let's summarize the usual approach for reducing the defiance of ODD children. The usual approach is 1) to build an alliance with the child, and 2) to develop a behavior modification system with your spouse and with your child's teachers. It is important to show a child who is used to arguing with adults that adults can be allies. Behavior modification will not usually work well with an ODD child if some adult does not also form a good alliance with him. When it is necessary to enforce rules, adults should take clear and concrete actions according to the behavior plan they devised, and avoid arguments with their child.

While these ideas are still useful for children who have been abused, there are additional strategies which are needed in cases of abuse. A long term relationship with a therapist is usually necessary so that the child can share his feelings about the abuse, and regain a sense of control over his life. For abused children, there needs to be a chance to talk about the pain they experienced. An abused child may be fearful of continued mistreatment by the abuser, or by other adults or even aggressive children. The child may blame himself or in some way misperceive why the abuse happened. In therapy, the child shares the full range of his feelings about the abuse: his fear, guilt, despair, and anger. The therapist listens, empathizes, and makes helpful observations. Over time, the painful feelings have less power in the child's mental life, and the child begins to feel free of the torture he endured. The child regains a sense of safety and confidence. Once this happens, the child will likely be less defiant, and strategies, like behavior modification techniques, are no longer needed. Try to find a therapist who has experience with abused children. Ask your doctor, clergy, or school what resources there are in your community.

In order to help rule out the possibility of abuse or some other traumatic event as a cause for your child's defiance, you should think about what was going on in your child's life around the time his defiant behavior began, even if the defiance started many years ago. Did your child show several signs of stress or anxiety at that time? Did your child have trouble sleeping, become scared of physical contact with some adults or children, worry about being away from you, become scared of the dark, or suddenly not want to be alone? If there were several signs of anxiety beginning around the time your child became defiant, then it is possible that your child's defiance is a reaction to some trauma he experienced.

However, keep in mind that anxiety symptoms alone are not enough to conclude that your child suffered a trauma, because there are many reasons why children become anxious, most of which are unrelated to abuse. So it is important for someone to talk with your child about what was happening in his life around the time he showed signs of anxiety or defiance to try to figure out what was going on. You could ask him whether anyone older has ever hurt or scared him, or you could ask even more directly whether someone ever touched his private parts or asked him to touch their private parts; however, many children are reluctant to talk about abuse due to their fear that the abuser will find out and hurt them, or due to their guilt. They may feel they brought it on in some way or that they should have been able to stop it. If you have a hunch that your child has been abused, you should consult with a mental health professional.

You can see that what you do to help your child varies based on the information collected during the diagnostic process. Even when we know that the diagnosis is ODD, there can be an alternate pathway by which the disorder developed, and this alternative pathway needs to be taken into account when developing your strategy. This illustrates why it is important to keep an open mind about a child's diagnosis and to determine whether anything traumatic has happened in your child's life.

Other Traumas That May Cause Defiance

Other kinds of unusual, but powerful events in a child's life include the death of a parent or relative who has been instrumental in the child's upbringing. Sometimes it is the death of a long time friend. Usually children exhibit feelings of sadness or anxiety when an important person passes away. However, sometimes there are also signs of anger and defiance. Anger is one way children may cope with a major loss. If the loss happened several years ago, you may think the child has adjusted to it by now. However, if your child's defiant behavior began at that time, then there is the possibility that the two are related.

If your child's defiance emerged for the first time at a certain age when someone close to him did die, it would be advisable to talk with your child about any losses at that time in his life, and see if any emotional memories emerge. Listen carefully, and if a memory of someone special comes to his mind, make a reflective comment like "That person was really special to you." Have your child share some of his memories with you. Remember that a child's grief does not always get expressed all at once, and can come out at different times over the years. Listen and empathize with his painful feelings. While talking about the loss can be helpful, it is not advisable to push your child to talk about his memories. Rather, let your child's feelings emerge when he chooses to bring them up. If one day your child is showing a lot of emotion in his face, such as tears, but not talking about his feelings, then I would recommend you gently ask your child about why he is emotional and see if he wants to talk.

While we are on the subject of past losses, I need to caution you again that not every painful event has long term effects on your child's behavior. Let's say that your child has experienced a significant loss or trauma. Do not jump to the conclusion that this is the cause of your child's defiance. The event may have nothing to do with your child's defiance today! What you thought might still be bothering your child might not really be a cause of his defiant behavior at all. Just as there are "red herrings" in detective work, there can be red herrings when we try to determine a child's diagnosis. I have worked with oppositional children who have lost parents, but the loss was not the cause of their oppositionality. The loss may be remembered with sadness, but the child's defiant nature was either formed before the loss, or developed some years after. Similarly, abuse can have profound effects on a child's life, but may not cause oppositionality.

How do you know whether a loss, or trauma, was instrumental in bringing about your child's defiant behavior? *What you should try to do is determine whether the child's defiance increased at the time of the loss or trauma.* During the six months following a loss, or during the time when abuse was occurring, did the child's attitude toward authority figures change? Did the child start challenging your rules? If he did not, then the loss or abuse is not likely the cause of the child's defiance, though it is still an issue to keep an eye on, because it could bring on some sadness or anxiety in your child's life. If the change in your child's behavior did occur around the time of the loss or trauma, then it will be important to talk about the trauma and help your child come to terms with it. Often a professional will be needed to help your child deal with the trauma. Your child's defiance may wane after the loss or trauma is addressed more fully.

Is the Cause Situational or Structural or Both?

There is another reason we may change our evaluation of the cause of a child's defiance: sometimes everyone is so focused on the current situational cause, that a more long term issue is overlooked at first. When we consider the present difficulties a child is having, the immediate situation may seem to be the primary cause. However, there may be other important causes that will become more obvious as time goes on. A child's headstrong personality or oppositional defiant disorder may emerge as a major cause once we observe the child over a longer period of time. In other cases, there may be a long term problem with the marriage or with a parent's personality which comes to light.

For example, a teenager's defiance may seem to be situational. Your teen may be mostly angry about his curfew because his peer group has a much later one. Or in the case of Felicia, her wish to spend more time with her boyfriend was due to her growing individuation from her family. However, there may have also been long term issues with defiance, which everyone overlooks at first because the recent events are so much worse than anything that occurred before.

It will usually become clear whether there are other long term issues once you begin to apply the strategies for the situational problem and find that the teen's defiance does not lessen significantly. For example, you offer compromises, and your teen finds fault with all of them, and is unwilling to bend at all. First, make sure that you are correctly applying the strategies for short term, developmental changes that occur during the teen years. Review the chapter on situational causes of defiance. Also, check with a friend or relative to see whether they can see anything amiss in your approach. If you think you are applying the approach correctly, then maybe the problem is greater than just a teenager struggling for independence.

You begin to realize that your teen has really been defiant for a very long time, even before becoming a teenager. Maybe you adapted to your child's argumentative personality in years past, and did not see it as a problem. Now you realize your child has been difficult to deal with for years. And you realize that you need to apply the strategies for oppositional defiant children, not just the strategies for situational defiance. You decide that you need to form a better alliance with your teenager, and you invite him to spend "down" time with you once a week at his favorite restaurant. You also show more interest in his activities, and maybe watch some DVDs together. You gradually develop a better rapport, and once that happens, you find you can talk with your teenager about his complaints and reach some compromises.

Maybe in your family there is a different long term problem. It is not that your teen has ODD, but that there has been a strain in your marriage for a long time, and that the marital problems are affecting your child. This could come to light as you work with your spouse on your teenager's demands. For example, consider the teen who wants to spend more time at night with his peer group. You try to set a reasonable curfew, and your spouse seems to agree, but when your child comes home late, your spouse does not back you up. Your spouse says it is not a big deal and undermines your authority with your teenager. This happens not just once, but several times. You realize that you and your spouse have been working at cross purposes when it comes to the rules for your teenager. In addition you may realize that you and your spouse have been spending less time together, and do not seem happy together. Unless you address your marital issues, it will be difficult to work together on your teenager's behavior.

Sometimes it is not a marital problem, but one parent's emotional issues that get in the way. In Felicia's case, it was the mother's emotional needs that were an additional factor making it difficult for her to compromise on a curfew. At first, it seemed the cause was just situational and not also due to the mother's emotional issues. The situational cause was Felicia's maturation and her wish to be closer to her peers. Felicia had a boyfriend who had a later curfew, and she wanted to spend more time with him. But Felicia's mother did not want to compromise at first on a later curfew. Why was it difficult for the mother to allow Felicia more time with her boyfriend? Upon further reflection, it became apparent that Felicia's mother had a close relationship with Felicia and did not want their relationship to change. She was used to spending time talking with her in the evenings at home, while her husband worked late. Once the mother recognized she was holding on too tight due to her own needs, she turned more to her spouse and her friends for companionship, and she decided to allow Felicia to stay out later with her boyfriend. A compromise was reached with her daughter, and the defiance waned.

Fetal Alcohol Spectrum Disorder

Another possible cause of defiant behavior, which may be overlooked in the evaluation process, is fetal alcohol spectrum disorder (FASD). It may not have occurred to you or your doctor to ask about the prenatal period of development, particularly if your child's behavior fits into a more common category, such as ADHD, oppositional defiant disorder, or bipolar disorder. In the case of adopted children, parents may not know to what extent the biological mother used alcohol or other drugs. However, if your child has had significant emotional and cognitive difficulties in addition to periods of defiant behavior throughout his life, then you should rule out alcohol or other drug effects that could have occurred during pregnancy. Embryos can develop serious central nervous system deficits if mothers drink excessively during pregnancy. Unfortunately, there can be lifelong cognitive and emotional deficits as a result. Sometimes the effects are obvious from birth, such as physical differences (e.g. facial features) and severe intellectual impairment (e.g. retardation). However, sometimes the effects on the central nervous system are not as obvious at birth, but still can have profound effects on the child's life.

One possible result can be behavioral problems, such as emotional outbursts, impulsivity, and social problems beginning at a young age. Attention deficits and learning disabilities may also be present. Parents remark that there are some days when their children refuse to go along with adult requests, and when their children become extremely angry if pushed to conform to adult rules. There can be rage reactions that last for an hour or more, similar to what is seen with bipolar children. It should be noted that not all FASD children have this problem, though. There is no one emotional or cognitive outcome for all children with fetal alcohol spectrum disorder. Some professionals propose that the effects on the child's brain depend on which trimester of pregnancy the mother drank to excess, as different parts of the central nervous system are developing more rapidly during different months of pregnancy. If you suspect a fetal alcohol disorder, you should consult with doctors who are familiar with this range of disorders. Your child will likely need a series of interventions, possibly including medication, psychotherapy, and special educational services.

Clues Which Indicate a "Hidden" Cause

In this chapter I have been describing cases of defiance where the true cause emerges over time. Usually, the diagnostic process which I outlined in chapters two though seven will lead you to discover the correct cause. However, sometimes a cause may have been "hidden" because there was an earlier trauma that has been submerged for one reason or another, or because one cause was so glaring that you overlooked other additional causes that have been contributing to your child's defiance. How will you know if there is a "hidden" cause besides the more obvious one? If you try the approach that was recommended in this book for the more obvious cause of your child's defiant behavior, and there is no change in your child's behavior, then go back over the diagnostic questions and see what else might be a cause of your child's defiance. Also, if your child's defiance has been going on for a long time, think again about when it started and see if you can remember anything else that might have affected your child at that time. Sometimes you will realize that an earlier loss or trauma might have brought about your child's defiant behavior. Consider also any possible prenatal effects, such as excessive alcohol and drug use by the mother during pregnancy.

Sometimes a clue that there could be a "hidden" cause may come from remarks made by your child or by another family member while you are applying one of the strategies from this book. Your child may say something that sheds light on the true underlying cause. For example, if you are imposing a behavioral strategy with consequences for incomplete school work, your child may say something like "I don't get this. This work is impossible." Now it could be that your child is trying to avoid responsibility for the missed assignment, but it is also possible your child is struggling because of a learning problem.

Remember the case of Donny who became argumentative with his parents and provocative with his older siblings, and they could not figure out why at first. He had been a compliant child up until recently. The cause seemed to be situational, but the parents could not figure out what had changed in Donny's life. Donny had not begun adolescence yet, so the cause was not a maturational change. Furthermore, the parents felt that nothing had changed in the family or at Donny's school. It was a comment by a friend of the mother which helped solve the puzzle. She remarked one day that the mother seemed so busy helping her older son apply to college. The mother and older son had been visiting a few colleges and were working on the applications together at night. The friend's observation helped the mother make the connection that maybe Donny was feeling a loss of her attention because the mother was busier with the older son. Once she began devoting more time to Donny, his attitude became less rebellious, and the problem was resolved.

You may have a hard time figuring out the cause at first. Keep your "detective" hat on and keep thinking about what might be underlying your child's behavior. Look over the key diagnostic questions, which are listed in the chart in chapter two. If on further reflection you think that one of these questions could apply to your child, then you should go back over the corresponding chapter in the book where that question is addressed. In the next chapter, I will tell you how to go about getting outside help for problems that are not getting any better.

Chart # 9.1: Re-evaluating the Cause

I.   **Past traumatic events can sometimes cause defiant behavior**

    A.   Marital discord or divorce

    B.   Physical or sexual abuse

    C.   Death of key relative or friend

II.   **Sometimes the situational cause is so glaring that the child's personality or the marital problems are overlooked at first.**

III. **Fetal alcohol spectrum disorder**

IV.   **How do you determine if there is a "hidden" cause of your child's defiance?**

    A.   Did your child's defiance begin around the time of a trauma?

    B.   If your current strategy is not working, review my diagnostic questions and look for signs that there is another cause for your child's behavior.

    C.   Your child, family member, or friend may make an off-handed remark which suggests a possible cause. Be open to other people's ideas.

Chapter 10

Resources for Parents

This book has introduced you to different possible causes of defiance in children. I hope you have figured out the cause of your child's defiance and have learned what you can do to help resolve conflict in your family. You may want additional help, and in this chapter I will point you in the right direction. First, I will offer suggestions about picking a mental health professional to help you and your family. Second, I will tell you about other books, organizations, and websites that provide information about the various diagnoses we have discussed in this book.

Picking the Right Therapist

A mental health professional can help you in several ways. This book has taught you how to figure out the cause of your child's defiance and has given you suggestions about what to do for each cause. You now have a direction and have begun addressing the cause of your child's defiance. However, you may still have questions about the diagnosis you came up with, and you may also want someone to help you address the problem with your child, your family, or the child's school. A therapist can answer questions you might have about your child's diagnosis and can help tailor an approach for your child. The therapist can give you specific advice about what to do for your child and your family. For example, if your child is headstrong, a mental health professional can help you develop a behavior plan to motivate your child to be more cooperative. Furthermore, for a child who has a personality disorder, like ODD, a mental health professional is often needed to form an alliance with your child in order for him to learn how to relate to adults as allies, rather than opponents. If your child develops a trusting relationship with a mental health professional, it will help your child learn to trust you and other adults.

Mental health professionals can help with the other causes of defiance as well. If the cause of defiance has to do with your marriage, then a marital therapist is often needed to help you break destructive patterns in your relationship with your spouse. If the cause is a mood disorder, like bipolar disorder, or if the cause is ADHD, then a psychiatrist is needed to prescribe the appropriate medication.

How do you determine which mental health professional to seek out for your child's problem? Mental health professionals have different kinds of training and experience. Psychiatrists are medical doctors who specialize in mental health. Most psychiatrists today perform evaluations and prescribe medications; few do psychotherapy. Psychologists on the other hand do evaluations and psychotherapy, but most cannot prescribe medication (with the exception of some psychologists who practice in states that allow them to obtain prescription privileges). Psychologists have a doctorate degree, either a Ph.D. or Psy.D. in psychology. Not all professionals who work with children have a doctorate degree. Other professionals who do psychotherapy with children and families include social workers and counselors. They hold master's degrees.

It is important to look into a therapist's clinical experience as well as their degree. Some doctors and therapists specialize in particular disorders or with particular age groups. Some professionals work primarily with adults, and others work primarily with children and their families. If you think the primary problem is with your marriage or with your own psychological issues, then choose a professional who works with adults. Some therapists who work with adults specialize in marital therapy and some in individual therapy. Be sure to ask what the professional's specialty is. Does it match what your needs are?

If you feel that your child has a headstrong personality, oppositional defiant disorder, or a mood disorder, you will want a therapist who meets with children. It will be important for the therapist to build an alliance with your child. It will also be helpful for the therapist to strategize with you about how to handle behavioral problems at home and in school. Sometimes the same therapist will perform both tasks, and sometimes the therapist will recommend one professional to work with your child and another to work with you. It is helpful to have two different therapists if your child is worried about his therapist sharing his thoughts with you, which is a concern especially of some adolescents. See what your therapist thinks would be best for your family.

Not to confuse you, but there is another possible way for a therapist to help your headstrong or oppositional child. That is to hold some meetings with the entire family together. These joint meetings allow the therapist to observe first hand the communication patterns in your family and to make suggestions that can impact everyone at the same time. Your other children will likely be invited to join, because they have a part in the interactions of the family. The child's siblings are often affected by the conflict in the family, and in addition they may have interesting observations about how you and your defiant child get along. In the case of Donny and Sam, the siblings made valuable contributions in family sessions about what was going wrong in the family.

Another kind of problem for which family therapy is especially helpful is when there is a situational stressor impacting everyone in the family. Family members can share how they have been affected by the stressor and how they are coping. A defiant child may learn he is not the only one upset with the change in the family's life and, in addition, the child may learn from other family members how to cope.

If there is the possibility of a learning disorder, you will want a psychologist who specializes in learning evaluations. After testing your child, the psychologist can meet with you and the teachers at your child's school in order to make recommendations to help your child with his learning problems. Another professional who could do a learning evaluation of your child is a school psychologist (who usually has a master's degree in school psychology). Many school districts employ school psychologists to do educational testing. You could ask your school to do a "case study evaluation", and as part of that evaluation the school psychologist will administer some tests to determine the type of learning problem your child might have. Some parents prefer a private evaluation, and others want the school to do the testing. The advantage of a school evaluation is that it is free. The advantage of a private evaluation is that it is often more thorough. Either way, once the evaluation is complete, you can share the recommendations with your child's teachers.

If your child has a mood disorder or ADHD and might benefit from medication, your child's therapist or family doctor may recommend a child psychiatrist (who has an MD). Some pediatricians and family doctors also are experienced with medications for ADHD and for mood disorders. However, most pediatricians and family doctors do not see many children with bipolar disorder, so that it would be advisable to consult with a child psychiatrist if you think your child might have bipolar disorder. If you work with both a psychiatrist and a therapist, ask them to consult with each other. The psychiatrist will benefit from the therapist's insights and vice versa.

Once you have read this book and figured out the likely cause of your child's problem, you will be better able to decide whether this is something you can deal with on your own, or whether you need professional help. If you decide to seek out a professional, look for someone who has experience with what you think is happening with your child. You will have an idea whether you need a psychologist to build an alliance with your child, or someone to advise you on behavior modification, or a psychologist who tests for learning disabilities, or a marital therapist, or maybe a physician to prescribe medication.

If you are unsure of the cause or if there are multiple causes, then you will want a professional who has worked with many different defiant children and their parents. The more experience a therapist has with children who exhibit defiance or anger, the more likely he will be able to help determine the cause of your child's problem. It is often helpful to get a recommendation from someone you trust: either another parent who has already accessed services in your town, a teacher at your child's school, or your child's pediatrician or family doctor. Ask which mental health professional has had success with defiant children.

Once you pick a professional to work with your child, how long should therapy take and how do you know if you are on the right path? It is tough to predict the length of therapy. Many structural causes of defiance will require months, or sometimes a year or more of psychotherapy. However, there are some signs to consider along the way to determine if you are on the right track. Your therapist should be able to develop a rapport with you and your child. Oppositional children will not always want to go to therapy at first, but after about five to ten sessions, your child should be less resistant, if not agreeable, about meeting with someone. Your child may make a comment like "He listens," or "She's OK," or "I don't need it, but I'll go."

It is also important that you, the parents, feel that the therapist has offered a plan that makes sense, and that the therapist keeps in touch with you. An exception would be if you have an older child who makes it clear that he does not want the therapist to meet with you because of confidentiality concerns, in which case you might be referred to a different therapist.

One way to evaluate the progress is to set some goals with the therapist at the start, and periodically assess progress in those areas with the therapist. One approach to setting goals would be to think about the situations when your child is most defiant (review the chart you used in chapter one), and set the goal as a decrease in frequency of defiant behavior in those situations. Over several months, you hope to observe some occasions where your child is cooperative, or at least not as defiant as he was at the start of therapy. That would be a sign that you are on the right track. However, it may take longer than a few months for your child to get along with you on a regular basis.

Other Books and Websites That Can Help

We have covered many different underlying problems that can cause defiance, and I want to refer you to other books where you can learn more about these problems. In chapter four I introduced you to autistic spectrum disorders and learning disabilities. Two good books for parents about autistic disorders are Tony Attwood's *Asperger's Syndrome*, published by Kingsley in London in 1998, and Chantal Sicile-Kira's *Autistic Spectrum Disorders*, published by Berkley in New York in 2004. Dr. Atwood's book focuses on strategies to help children with one type of autistic disorder called Asperger's, while Ms. Sicile-Kira's book provides an overview of the range of autistic disorders. Ms. Sicile-Kira's book also refers you to other resources, including books written by older children who have autistic disorders. If your child has a form of autism, it may be helpful to read about how someone else coped with the disorder.

In the area of learning disorders, a good place to start is with the books by Mel Levine, a pediatrician who writes clearly about different kinds of learning disabilities. A book written for children ages approximately ten and up is Dr. Levine's *Keeping A Head in School*, published in 1990 by Educator's Publishing in Cambridge. It explains which brain (or cognitive) functions are used for different academic tasks. Dr. Levine's book *A Mind at a Time* is written for parents and was published in 2002 by Simon and Schuster in New York. This book reviews various learning problems in more detail, and explains how to help your child develop his cognitive abilities.

For books on discipline techniques for headstrong children, I would recommend Thomas Phelan's *1-2-3 Magic*, published in 1995 by Child Management in Glen Ellyn, Illinois, and also Robert Eimers and Robert Aitchison's *Effective Parent, Responsible Children*, published in 1977 by McGraw-Hill in New York. Both books explain how to implement a behavioral strategy that rewards self-control and that imposes negative consequences for oppositional behaviors.

In the area of childhood disorders, we touched on ADHD. There are many books written on this subject, and I will refer you to three. Edward Hallowell and John Ratey wrote *Driven to Distraction*, which was published by Touchstone in New York in 1994. It gives the reader a clear idea of how ADHD affects a person's life from childhood to adulthood.

Russell Barkley's *Taking Charge of ADHD* published by Guilford in New York in 2000 looks at both the causes and treatments of ADHD. Finally, David Gottlieb, Tom Shoaf, and Risa Graff co-wrote *Why is My Child's ADHD Not Better Yet? Recognizing the Undiagnosed Secondary Conditions That may be Affecting Your Child's Treatment*, which was published in 2006 by McGraw-Hill in New York. About 70% of children with ADHD have one or more additional disorders, and Dr. Gottlieb explains how to identify each of the common secondary conditions. The authors also point out the various treatment options for children who have ADHD and an additional disorder, including oppositional defiant disorder and bipolar disorder.

For children who do not have ADHD but who show signs of oppositional defiant disorder or conduct disorder, two books that give helpful suggestions to parents are Russell Barkley and Christine Benton's *Your Defiant Child* published by Guilford in New York in 1998, and Ross Greene's *The Explosive Child* published by HarperCollins in New York in 2001. Dr. Barkley and Ms. Benton as well as Dr. Greene give useful strategies for developing rapport with oppositional children and for lessening conflict.

One of the first books for parents about bipolar disorder in children was written by Dr. Demitri Papolos and Janice Papolos. It is called *The Bipolar Child*, and was published by Broadway Books in New York in 1999. It helps parents understand the diagnosis and explains various biological approaches to the disorder. *An Unquiet Mind*, by Kay Jamison, is a first person account of what it is like to have bipolar disorder. Though most of the book is about her adult life, Dr. Jamison also writes a section about her childhood. The book is an honest and moving account of how she overcame her illness to become a respected psychiatrist.

I would like to recommend a couple of good books if there are problems in your marriage. Dr. Harriet Lerner's *The Dance of Anger*, published by HarperCollins in New York in 1985, helps couples understand what underlies their conflicts. *Fighting for Your Marriage*, written by Drs. Howard Markham, Scott Stanley and Susan Blumberg, was published by John Wiley in San Francisco in 2001. It gives practical suggestions for reducing conflict and building rapport with your spouse.

Before moving on to resources on the web, I want to mention a few books about child abuse. Dave Pelzer has written several books about how he endured severe physical abuse and neglect by his mother. *A Child Called It: One Child's Courage To Survive* is an autobiographical account of his childhood and was published in 1995 by Health Communications of Deerfield Beach, Florida. An excellent book written for adults who have been sexually abused is *The Sexual Healing Journey* by Wendy Maltz. This book was published in 1991 by HarperCollins. Finally, Cynthia Crosson-Tower has written a textbook *Understanding Child Abuse and Neglect*, which has separate sections about physical abuse, neglect, and sexual abuse of children. Each chapter also contains a list of references for further reading. The seventh edition was published in 2007 by Allyn and Bacon.

Regarding help on the web, I'd recommend you check the sites of these organizations: NAMI (National Alliance on Mental Illness) is a national, mental health support group that can be found at www.nami.org; and NIMH (National Institute of Mental Health) is the main government agency focusing on mental health, which is at www.nimh.nih.gov. Both sites give current information about a number of mental health issues.

There is also information about different psychological problems on the site of the American Psychological Association at www.apa.org. Another professional organization, the American Psychiatric Association, has a site www.healthyminds.org which includes the names of parent support groups for various emotional disorders in children. Some of the support groups have local chapters where you could attend meetings with other families.

Parent networks online offer practical suggestions for different kinds of problems, including mental health issues. One useful network is the Berkeley Parents Network, which is at www.parents.berkeley.edu.

Here are some useful sites for learning disabilities and attention problems in children. In the area of learning disabilities, check out LD Online at www.ldonline.org. For help with ADHD, the national support group · CHADD (Children and Adults with Attention Deficit/Hyperactivity Disorder) has a site www.chadd.org.

If you are looking for help finding residential schools for children with mental health disorders, two useful sites are the National Association of Therapeutic Schools and Programs www.natsap.org, and the Boarding School Review at www.boardingschoolreview.com.

Made in the USA
San Bernardino, CA
26 January 2015